Truganinni

3 WORKSHOP PLAYS

BILL REED

Published by Reed Independent, Melbourne, 2015

First published 1977 by Heinemann Educational Australia Pty Ltd as part of its Australian Theatre Workshop series, ISBN 0858591502

Printed by Createspace.com, a division of Amazon.com

Available as a printed book or an ebook from Createspace.com or Amazon.com or Kindle estores, together with most major international online outlets or bookshops with online ordering facilities

Copyright © Bill Reed 1977

Re-issue cover: Dilani Priyangika Ranaweera, Dart Lanka Productions, Colombo, Sri Lanka

National Library of Australia Cataloguing-in-Publication entry
Creator: Reed, Bill - author.
Title: Truganinni: three workshop plays/ Bill Reed.
Edition: Second edition.
ISBN: 9780994280596 (paperback)
Subjects: Truganini, 1812?-1876 -- Drama.
Aboriginal Tasmanians -- Drama.
Australian drama -- 20th century.
Dewey Number: A822.3

National Library of Australia Cataloguing-in-Publication entry
Creator: Reed, Bill -- author.
Title: Truganinni: three workshop plays/ Bill Reed.
Edition: Second edition.
ISBN: 9780994322708 (ebook)
Subjects: Truganini, 1812?-1876--Drama.
Aboriginal Tasmanians -- Drama.
Australian drama -- 20th century.
Dewey Number: A822.3

Truganinni

3 WORKSHOP PLAYS

BILL REED

Other works by Bill Reed
The Pipwink Papers\
Me, the Old Man
Stigmata
Ihe
Dogod
Crooks
Tusk
Throw her back
Are You Human?
Tasker Tusker Tasker
Awash
1001 Lankan Nights book 1
1001 Lankan Nights book 2
Water Workout (Nonfiction)

plays
Burke's Company
Truganinni
The Pecking Order
Mr Siggie Morrison with his Comb and Paper*
Jack Charles is Up and Fighting
Just Out of Your Ground
You Want It, Don't You, Billy?
I Don't Know What to Do with You!
Paddlesteamer
Cass Butcher Bunting
More Bullsh
Talking to a Mirror
Auntie and the Girl

award-winning short stories *(see title 'Passing Strange')*
Messman on the C.E. Altar
English Expression
The 200-year Old Feet
The Case Inside
Blind Freddie Among the Pickle Jars
The Old Ex-serviceman
Mahood on the Thin Beach
The Shades of You my Dandenong

CONTENTS

First Production 1

Truganinni the Lady 3

Part 1: White Exercises 5

Part 2: Pantagruel In-between 35

Part 3: King Billy's Bones 75

To any happier memory of Truganinni that might be left.

FIRST PRODUCTION

Truganinni was first performed at The Union Theatre, University of Melbourne, April, 1970, with the following creative team:

Part 1: White Exercises

TASMANIAN WOMAN   Rose Lynorin
WHITE MAN   Stephen Waters
MANGANA   Tom Healy
WONGGU   Michael Myer
TRUGANINNI   Jan Hamilton
GUDJARA   Des Fitzgerald
MR MELLIN   Robert Lewers
MRS MELLIN   Meredith Rogers
LOWE   Bill Saw
NEWELL   David Johnson

Part 2: Pantagruel In-between

GEORGE AUGUSTUS ROBINSON   Guthrie Worby
REVEREND DOVE   Ian McFadyen
BOB   Derek James
MRS CLARK   Marg Jacobs
SCOTTISH INSPECTOR   Patrick Farrell
BRITISH INSPECTOR   Howard Parkinson
ACHILLES   Andrew Webb
APHRODITE   Alison French
CONSTITUTION   John Jacobs
PIANIST   Martin Arnold

Part 3: King Billy's Bones

ALEXANDER McKAY   Ian Robinson
GILET   Derek James
DR DINGBY   Jan Martin

(continued overpage)

MILLINGTON Jeff Curtis
MOLLY   Roslyn Horin
COLVIN   Dennis Howard
TIMMS   Michael Myer
ATWELL   John Price

DIRECTOR   George Whaley
SET DESIGNER   Jan Martin
COSTUME DESIGN   Sasha Soldatow
STAGE MANAGER   Alex Craig
LIGHTING   Ric Hunter
SOUND   Martin Arnold
SET CONSTRUCTION   Russell Stafford

TRUGANINNI THE LADY

'She was the daughter of Mangana, Chief of Bruni Island. Later in life, when she had mastered English, she told her story to Alexander McKay. Her mother was stabbed to death by a European. Her sister was carried off by sealers. In her childhood, accompanied by her intended husband Paraweena and another man, she was once on the mainland of Van Diemans Land. Two sawyers, Lowe and Newell, undertook to row the party to nearby Bruni Island. In mid-channel, the white men threw the natives overboard. As they struggled and grasped the gunwale, Lowe and Newell chopped off their hands with hatchets. The mutilated Aborigines were left to drown and the Europeans were free to do as they pleased with the girl.'

Clive Turnbull, 'The Black War'

'... For example, the Tasmanian Aborigines died out not just because they were hunted like kangaroos for an afternoon's sport, but also because a world in which this could happen was intolerable to them; so they committed suicide as a race by refusing to breed. Ironically perhaps, and as though to confirm the Aborigines' judgement, the mummified remains of the old lady who was the last to survive have been preserved as a museum curiosity.'

A. Alvarez, 'The Savage God'

'Seven years after King Billy's death, Truganinni stood alone, a living relic of her race. She would walk the streets of Hobart Town, resembling Queen Victoria in her voluminous skirts and headdress. She quite enjoyed the curiosity and finger pointing of the townspeople.

Towards the end, she appeared to bear no malice towards her race's persecutors. Growing stoutish, she smoked a pipe and enjoyed a daily jug of beer. But she began to grow ill and as her death loomed, so did the memories of what happened to King Billy's body.

The fear obsessed her like a disease and repeatedly she begged and pleaded that no such horror should befall her.

On May 8th 1876, at the approximate age of 73, Truganinni died.

Only hours after the news, body-snatchers in the Royal Society of Tasmania started to bark for her body. The government tried to fight them off.

She was buried in a secret grave in a plain wooden casket. But the promises made to her were false ones, yet again. Years after her death her body was exhumed with the full approval of the government. Her skeleton was displayed in the Tasmanian Museum, alongside the skeletons of animals.

In 1953, a deputation to the Tasmanian Premier resulted in her skeleton being removed from public display and placed in a box to be opened only by 'bona fide' scientists.

And thus it was that, for decades, in a black casket in Hobart's Tasmanian Museum lay the broken bones of an aboriginal queen – and in her irreverent tomb are squashed the broken dreams of a race.'

Tess Lawrence, Melbourne Herald, 24 May 1974

Author's note: In 2002, there came an official public burial of sorts. Some of her 'hair and flesh' that had been lodged with the College of Surgeons in London were returned to Tasmania, allowing a formal ceremony before the nation's cameras of scattering her ashes on the waters of her beloved Derwent.

Play 1: WHITE EXERCISES

PRODUCTION NOTE

Play 1 is a play for masks. It is not intended as a play in which the actors try to crop a realism artificially out of the Tasmanian Aborigines' culture or language.

It is a play that should be treated in what resembles workshop production -- that is to say, one that presents the theatrical illusion as nothing more or nothing less than the theatrical illusion that is inherent in the actors' masks.

Some 'rhythm sequences' need only be spoken in rhythm, while others should be accompanied by actors beating rhythm sticks. Rhythms can begin sharply or can build up slowly -- but they should always end abruptly and dramatically.

It is suggested that Play 1 should take place with actors moving centrally from sitting around the periphery of an 'acting area'. No exits or entrances, only rhythmic pauses and changes of pace.

Play 1: LIST OF CHARACTERS

TASMANIAN WOMAN
WHITE MAN
MANGANA, chief of the Bruni tribe
WONGGU, Tasmanian
TRUGANINNI, daughter of Mangana
GUDJARA, the songman
MELLIN, Superintendent
MRS MELLIN, his wife
LOWE, a white sawyer
NEWELL, a white sawyer
CHORUS, as necessary

Scene 1

(A group of actors are seated about the stage as the audience enters. They chat, move as they like. Finally they pick up rhythm sticks and begin to use them, experimenting individually or in twos or threes. They join into larger groups as the sound builds up to one solid rhythm.

Silence... actors freeze. One of the actresses puts on a black mask and rises. She moves to central area and mimes digging movement.

Renewed rhythm, and one of the actors in a white mask rises and edges up to her. As his shadow falls over her, she jumps up, screaming silently, and tries to escape. He catches her, beats her into submission, and rapes her. Then gets up, looks down at her, bends down as if in tenderness or sympathy, and then simply stabs her in the back. With shame or guilt he simply returns to the circle.

Renewed silence.

Two actors don black masks as MANGANA and WONGGU. They see the dead woman. MANGANA falls onto the woman's body in grief. Finally they carry her back to the circle.

Rhythm again.

Actor as white man walks to front of stage, with his back to WONGGU, who stalks him and, with slow determination, strikes him with his waddy. The white man falls. Down stage, an actor jumps up and assumes a shooting pose. He shoots; all hit their sticks hard. WONGGU falls.

MANGANA crosses to WONGGU. TRUGANINNI is behind him. He looks down at the body for a long time, then picks up a spear. The white man takes up a shooting pose.

In silence again. Long pause.

MANGANA lets the spear fall, picks up the body and, dignity lost, moves slowly away. He walks backward with slow formal steps. TRUGANINNI, bewildered, picks up the spear and follows her father.

Rhythm very slow rhythm begins as MANGANA and TRUGANINNI ceremoniously return the body to the circle. Defeated, MANGANA walks back to the elevated position in central area, where he remains for the duration of Play 1.

His manner throughout is one of having given up all hope. He freezes in position as rhythm builds up. Rhythm changes and TRUGANINNI stands up. TRUGANINNI runs over to MANGANA. Stops. Pause. Then approaches her father reverently, offering food)

TRUGANINNI: The roots of our earth, father. Our people sent them over. For these roots, they said my father will come back into our camp...
(pause)
I told them I did not think so.
(pause)
I worked for these, too. Will you eat them?

MANGANA: (desultory)   Yes, Truganinni.

TRUGANINNI: Tomorrow, I shall dig with my mother's stick. Today I wanted to work with my hands for you.

MANGANA: I will eat.

TRUGANINNI: Tomorrow there will be more.

(Pause)

MANGANA: (looking around) You have come alone. Where is your sister? Where is Gudjara?

TRUGANINNI: Gudjara is coming. He follows me everywhere.

MANGANA: Gudjara is my friend.

(In rhythm now)

TRUGANINNI: Why does he follow? Always follow?

MANGANA: Gudjara is your kin, and I told him to.

TRUGANINNI: He is an old man. It tires him out.

MANGANA: Where is your sister?

TRUGANINNI: (giggles) I think Jalmarida is in love.

MANGANA: Where is she?

TRUGANINNI: Down on the shore, she watches footprints until they come up to her. I think she is in love.

(The rhythm-stick beats stop again)

MANGANA: She will come to see me!

TRUGANINNI: Now you are angry.

MANGANA: Have you seen her?

(Pause)

TRUGANINNI: No.

MANGANA: Where has she gone?

TRUGANINNI: Down by the water. I have told you.

(Rhythm sticks up again)

MANGANA: She doesn't come to see me. Something is wrong. Last night I heard a scream from over there. It was her. It was your sister.

TRUGANINNI: My sister screamed.

MANGANA: Why? You tell me why.

   Build up rhythm)

TRUGANINNI: She held her body and said, 'Something has gone in'. The old women laughed. The men threw dirt on her, and danced around. When she had screamed, she went to the fire and burnt herself.
  (pause)
Father, I am afraid!

MANGANA: No, no. Be careful only.

TRUGANINNI: I am afraid, father! Why does Gudjara follow, follow? No women go out to dig any more. No men with their spears. The men should hunt. I am young, but I am your daughter. I know there is something wrong!

MANGANA: They need not hunt now. They stand by the hut; the food is given.

  (Sudden stoppage of the rhythm sticks)

TRUGANINNI: What I remember does not happen anymore. The hunt, the chase, the food from the stick... even the old man Gudjara only follows me, a girl.

MANGANA: You tell my people to come over here.

TRUGANINNI: My mother died here.

MANGANA: Tell them.

TRUGANINNI: They won't

MANGANA: (suddenly tired)   Tell them.

  (Rhythm sticks up again)

TRUGANINNI: I have told them, father. There is no food over here, only my mother. They say before long you will have to go back there too. They wait there for you.

MANGANA: Say I tell them.

TRUGANINNI: There is no hut over here. The old women say they would have to go back to hunting and the white fellows would shoot them. Like my uncle, my mother. My mother. Why do they say that?

MANGANA: They are right.

TRUGANINNI: NO!

> *(Rhythm sticks stop.*
>
> *In the silence, MANGANA swirls his spear above his head, slams it down on the rostrum. Pace change. No rhythm sticks but spoken rhythm)*

MANGANA: Listen, Truganinni. Around, all around, the land that was once ours is now of no use. The white man numbers go on. Each time we went out, our land had got smaller, and two or three of us would not return. Why should they hunt?

TRUGANINNI: We ought to live!

MANGANA: They are too many. The whisperings are great.

TRUGANINNI: The shadows are long, cold winds from the south.

> *(Slow build-up of rhythm once more)*

MANGANA: The whisperings, the whisperings, the cold winds from the south.

> *(Pause)*

TRUGANINNI: (outcry) *What I remember does not happen anymore!*

(GUDJARA, the songman, moves into the central area)

GUDJARA: (pointing to TRUGANINNI) Ah. You.

TRUGANINNI: You leave me alone.

GUDJARA: You go too fast. I shall bring my son Paraweena, along. You would soon slow down for him.

TRUGANINNI: (crossly) When we are married.

GUDJARA: That's why he does not come with me. He does not care either.

TRUGANINNI: (quickly) Where is he?

GUDJARA: (laughing) Oh yes, you would soon slow down for him.

TRUGANINNI: You leave me alone.

GUDJARA: Mangana...

MANGANA: (shaking head) I am going to stay here. They all should come here to me. Once, they would have run behind.

GUDJARA: It's you who have left our people. Come back. They need your counsel.

(Sudden silence from the rhythm sticks, replaced by a slow build up of low hissing)

MANGANA: Now other whisperings are great. Greater. They have new counsellors now.

GUDJARA: These are not Mangana's.

MANGANA: My wife was broken where I now sit. They then looked for my counsel, and then I told them nothing. Wonggu is dead doing what I said. There can be no more counsel from me. Other whisperings, I say, are greater.

GUDJARA: They don't know that.

MANGANA: They must learn or they are going to die.

(hissing stops)

GUDJARA: But they are lost like children. There was a fight last night. And a spearing. A woman has not come back. The new white man with the food spoke to them sharply. They are children now.

MANGANA: New man? Another?

GUDJARA: He asked for you.

MANGANA: He will come to me.

(Rhythm stick build-up again)

GUDJARA: Come back, old friend. You only sit here alone.

MANGANA: At night, alone, my wife comes back to me.

(Pause)

GUDJARA: Are we dying?

(Rhythm sticks 'die' slowly)

MANGANA: Our land gets smaller, whispering, whispering. Soon where can we go?

(Pause.

During the following, it is suggested that TRUGANINNI and GUDJARA perform a fantasy hunt, with the old man tracking her and she finally falls pretend-exhausted.

The rhythms following their mime stop)

GUDJARA:

The old pig-rat licks his mouth, his paws.
His mouth, his paws, the old pig-rat licks.
Licking, licking, his old coat shines;
Turning his eyes looking for home
The old pig-rat bends looking for home.
For the old sun shines high in his eyes,
Turning his head, the old sun now shines –
Pig-rat filled with the yearning for home.
Across the grey plains, the pig-rat plains,
He looks for home, licking his old mouth,
But the old sun shines high in his eyes
The old sun shines high in his eyes.
Now the new sun only looks towards home;
The new sun only. The old pig-rat is dead.
The pig-rat is dead, and the new sun shines
The new sun shines on the death in his eyes.

(In the ensuing silence, the actors are still.

Finally:)

MANGANA: Last night, my daughter Jalmarida screamed.

GUDJARA: She will be back.

MANGANA: Where has she gone?

TRUGANINNI: I don't know!

MANGANA: (to her) I have asked Gudjara to follow you. You listen to him.

TRUGANINNI: (runs off, laughing) That old man will have to climb trees!

(GUDJARA chases her. They circle and finally drop back into the actors' circle, laughing. They stop suddenly. Freeze.)

Scene 2

(MANGANA adopts a new position. The Supervisor of Aborigines and his wife, MR and MRS MELLINS, stand up formally. They walk tentatively towards MANGANA.

Note: They and MANGANA speak point-counterpoint to each other by way of indicating the difficulty of communication. Either party tries much anyway...)

MRS MELLIN: It's him, James.

MELLIN: His spirit must be broken to sit here like this.

MANGANA: What do you want?

MRS MELLIN: What did he say?

MELLIN: (at him) I have heard of Mangana.

MRS MELLIN: Funny, I expected much more. You know what people say about him, James.

MELLIN: My name is Mellin. This is my wife. I'm here to help you, Mangana. You can come to me.

MRS MELLIN: Don't promise too much, James. Be the Supervisor. Try to think what would this one think of you if he could understand what you're saying? Let's not show weakness right off.

MANGANA: What do you want? Speak and go.

MRS MELLIN: What was that? I don't like the look of him. I'm sure he's just insulted us. Say something right back from the start.

MANGANA: (annoyed) What do you want?

MRS MELLIN: We can't have this tone, James. Tell him.

MELLIN: (ignoring her) You won't have heard of me as I have of you. These days your people live quietly. All Hobart Town knows that that is due to Mangana.

MRS MELLIN: Look at the brute's scars.

MELLIN: There have been one or two cases. A shooting, a waddying, but nothing like war. Due to Mangana. I am pleased, so I know what you go through to sit here like this. Too many white men speaking against you.

MRS MELLIN: Get on with it, James.

MELLIN: (stilt ignoring her) For my part here, more than the prayers and the rations, I'm here to keep the scum away. It's common knowledge what they come for. While I'm here, they'll keep away.

>*(gets no reply. The wife has gone impertinently close to examine MANGANA's face, but MELLINS doesn't bother to stop her... wouldn't think to)*

MANGANA: (eyes turned on him) You ask me a question as young as you are. Ask it of your kinsmen who come here at night. If you look, new man, you will see them creeping, wanting from us. You know what they want. We know what they want. We could kill them, as they have us.

MELLIN: Mangana, understand. I have more to give, and I'll see my methods tried.

MRS MELLIN: He should tell his people not to associate with such riff raff. Don't forget the details, the rations, James.

MELLIN: (simply) What would he care about those?

MRS MELLIN: (vexed) Mister Mangana, the question of your rations. I notice that there hasn't been very much order. The door has been rushed and the meat scrambled over. Even more than that, some of you have been coming up twice. Even given the difficulty in spelling your names, don't think I haven't noticed. Therefore, it would be appreciated if a queue were formed not before nine on Tuesdays, and no earlier than church for the Sabbath hand-out. It would also help if proper Christian names were used, or the savages were somehow distinctively marked. As there are now approximately fifty-two of you, the daily ration will be as follows: 3 lbs of fresh meat, 5 lbs of salted meat, 1 lb of biscuits and 4 lbs of potatoes. I trust that proper arrangements can be made for the betterment of all.

(Pause)

MANGANA: Your wife talks, new man. But I think you are able to talk with me.

MELLIN: My name is Mellin.

MANGANA: Mell-in. You hand out the food, and my people need not hunt. But I think we can talk.

MELLIN: I'm a law-abider, Mangana.

MANGANA: I will not look towards you, for you are only one man. There will be a time when your people will kill all of mine. My daughter Jalmarida is missing. She went off alone.

(He turns away, shuts off)

MELLIN: One last thing. This morning I met a sealer on this side of the straits. He is well known to me as a ruffian. There was a girl with him. She was from here, the camp. I caught them together on the sand, but when I tried to bring her back, she said no. I have no power to prevent him from taking her away if he wants to. Mangana?

MRS MELLIN: Deaf ears, James. Frankly I doubt whether it would even matter to him. Put it in your report. Only cover yourself, James. I keep telling you. It's enough that you should have volunteered for all this.

MELLIN: I happened to believe in this.

MRS MELLIN: Yes, yes. But only cover yourself, dear. That's what reports are for.

(The MELLINS return to the circle. Rhythm builds up to herald TRUGANINNI's entrance to centre)

MANGANA: Where is your sister?

TRUGANINNI: Looking. They are looking for her.

MANGANA: Then you stay here.

TRUGANINNI: Why must you worry? Gudjara will find her. That old man is crafty.

MANGANA: You stay here.

(Pause.

There is tension between them, which is highlighted by a burst from the rhythm sticks)

TRUGANINNI: (angry) Can I sit her like my father does?

MANGANA: You do not understand.

(Rhythm slows)

TRUGANINNI: You said we must live how they want or not live at all. Some are bad, yes, father. My mother died here. But I have been thinking. Why should I stay afraid? I walk and run and speak as before. I can dig where I was taught; the roots are still there. The wombat still peers from the dark hole, wanting to escape. My hand can move quickly if I really want to catch him. Why must I go with Gudjara, always afraid?

(Build up of rhythm)

MANGANA: You will listen to me.

TRUGANINNI: I cannot be afraid all the time. How will you eat? You won't take the food they give from the hut.

MANGANA: Sit here quiet.

TRUGANINNI: (stamping foot) How will you eat?

MANGANA: Wait for Gudjara.

TRUGANINNI: They are not all bad, these people. Have you not changed yourself, father? When do you hunt now? Why does my father not hunt now?

(Renewed silence; all waiting for answer)

MANGANA: Is that what my people are saying?

TRUGANINNI: (softly) Yes, father.

MANGANA: While they eat the white man's food.

TRUGANINNI: They are not happy. They want my father as he was.

MANGANA: They roll over on full bellies, and feel their fathers looking scornfully down on them. Then they speak like that. Only then. It is talk, Truganinni. Talk. You tell them, Mangana says, one day perhaps the white fellow will go on by as he came. The sea will draw him back to it again. Until then, we must wait. Who will sing of their going if we have all died? It is useless to talk. They must wait. You tell them. When Gudjara comes back.

TRUGANINNI: But why should I stay afraid of all white men? There are two who have spoken to Paraweena. Two who take wood from our land. They told Paraweena they don't want to do it or hurt us, but they have to live as other white men say. They told him they would give him and me things if we helped them carry the wood.

MANGANA: You will stay here!

TRUGANINNI: It is only to help them. We have said yes.

MANGANA: No!

TRUGANINNI: (petulant) How can they be bad? They are young like Paraweena. They look at me and I think they smile.

MANGANA: (strikes her) No!

(Pause. A rhythm stoppage)

MANGANA: (remorsefully) Truganinni, sing. Sing, Truganinni. Listen. It is your mother. Let us bring her here. Sing, sing your mother, for I get so old...

TRUGANINNI: (threnody)
Why do you sit here every day at my grave?
Why do you sit here? The shadows, the night,
The time comes to dance. The moon bone rises.
Why do you sit here every day at my grave?

MANGANA:
Because your body has been burnt and is ready;
The place of your bones is prepared by me.
I am Mangana; you remember your husband.
Mangana, your husband, prepared your bones.

TRUGANINNI:
Why do you sit here every day at my grave?
The place is prepared and I take my rest.

MANGANA:
Come up with your husband, come with me.
Get up from that place. Your husband speaks.
I saw you dancing there just now
I saw you leap when you spoke to me.
Get up from that grave. Your husband speaks.
Come with me, come with your husband.

TRUGANINNI:

You come down here and keep me warm
For I must dance to keep myself warm.
You should rub my body and slap my loins.
You ought not sit there while your wife is dancing.

MANGANA:
My old legs are cold, I shall warm you soon.

TRUGANINNI:
Your wife dances to keep herself warm,
Until you come, I shall keep myself warm...
Will you slap my loins to keep me warm?
My husband, Mangana, will you keep me warm?

MANGANA:
I sit here at your grave. My legs are old;
How shall I prepare you who has died so soon?
My wife, my wife, I shall keep you warm.

TRUGANINNI:
Where I dance is a dry and waterless place.
I am taking you to a dry and waterless place.

MANGANA:
Mangana comes with you to the waterless place...

(End rhythm; action freeze.

GUDJARA enters slowly, others wait for him to speak)

GUDJARA: I could not find Jalmarida.

MANGANA: She is lost.

GUDJARA: She went down to the water and took some flowers. They say she would not speak to anyone. Now she is gone.

TRUGANINNI: She will come back. Father? Gudjara? If I go for a walk and you cannot find me, will you say this about me too?

GUDJARA: She ran, old friend. She was running then away from us. I could see she was going somewhere.

TRUGANINNI: No. She is young like me. She climbed a tree and watched you go by. Now she sleeps and waits for me. She will come back.

GUDJARA: Her tracks stop at the water.

TRUGANINNI: She is waiting, waiting!

GUDJARA: No, Truganinni, I can see.

TRUGANINNI: (softly) She is waiting for me.

(Rhythm from the sticks builds up again for:)

CHORUS:
She has gone from us,
Where has she gone?
We sit here and wait but Jalmarida is gone.
Jalmarida is gone;
She is gone from us.

GUDJARA:
Crossing the water, she is running there
Wearing the waistband of her mother's hair.
She stops by the wattle
Yellow flowers spreading in her mother's hair.

CHORUS:
She is gone from us;
Where does she go?
We sit here and wait but Jalmarida is gone...

(CHORUS and rhythm sticks fade. Silence. TRUGANINNI and GUDJARA return slowly to circle

One hit with rhythm sticks is followed by lamenting rhythm and chanting.

LOWE and NEWELL don white masks. MELLIN enters and stops short seeing them do this)

LOWE: Listen to that black-hearted thump-thumping, will you? It's wicked, that is.

NEWELL: It is, but who cares?

LOWE: Nights are for blacks, Paddy. I'll see them in the day, I will.

NEWELL: Come on, will you?

LOWE: I'm for waiting, man. I don't like the sound of it. There'll be a chance, another.

NEWELL: I'm hot, Lowe, I'm telling you.

LOWE: They won't let us come near with that noise on. Nights are for blacks, Paddy.

NEWELL: I'll cut a few throats if they try anything. I'm hot, boyo, I'm telling you that. I've seen some of their women run, boyo.

LOWE: Man, we're friendly with a few. We'd best be waiting. We'll go back on chains if we're caught out on this.

NEWELL: They stole an axe from us. Get it? An axe. We're looking for it, see.

LOWE: We'll be back on dragging chains.

NEWELL: Not us. Come on, will you?

(They start to move off)

MELLIN: Stop, you!

LOWE: Christ!

MELLIN: Don't try running. I've seen your faces.

NEWELL: And who would you be, cock?

MELLIN: I'll have your back torn for this.

LOWE: He's the new lad running this place. That's who he is, Paddy.

NEWELL: Now what would he want to be yelling at us for, I'm asking you.

MELLIN: While I'm in charge here, your kind will keep away. Now, get off!

NEWELL: (menacingly) Minding our own bloody business, see, and you raising your voice. Did you hear him, Lowe? He wants to see us whipped, does he?

LOWE: Bloody rude, boyo. It's dark now, see.

MELLIN: (raising whip) Scum!

(They back away, but not fully and are menacing)

NEWELL: There's no good in losing your temper, gov.

LOWE: Come on, Paddy.

NEWELL: He won't be writing a report, will he?

MELLIN: They could hang you all and I'd sleep easy.

NEWELL: We came here for a bit of business. Business, we're telling you. A few trees. What else does he think?

(MRS MELLIN comes in tentatively)

MRS MELLIN: James...?

MELLIN: It's me.

MRS MELLIN: God, James, listen to them. That racket they're making. It's like the howling of wild animals. You left me alone.
(then)
What's the matter?

MELLIN: I'm not alone.

LOWE: Don't be alarmed, missus.

MRS MELLIN: Who are these people?

NEWELL: We've got some business with one of the blacks, missus. We work with our hands during the day, y'see, so we had to come about it now. We're telling you. But your hubby, he won't listen.

MRS MELLIN: You get out of here!

NEWELL: But we've got business. One of them, we've come to see him about it.

MRS MELLIN: And who might that be?

LOWE: Paraweena. Isn't it so, Paddy.

NEWELL: That's who it is. We cut wood. That black told us he'd help to get our wood across the estuary, Missus. We'd be paying him n' all. We need a hand tomorrow, and that's a fact.

LOWE: We were just holding back, like you, missus. Hair on the back of our necks. Like you, Missus.

MRS MELLIN: James, there *is* such a creature on our list. Paraweena. He's a young man, usually with that girl Truganinni or whatever.

LOWE: He won't believe us, missus.

MELLIN: They'd tear you to pieces if you went in there tonight. Now get out and come back in the light when I can see you.

MRS MELLIN: Don't be too hard, James.

NEWELL: He's a violent man, your hubby is, missus. Come on, Lowe.
   (over shoulder at MELLIN)
You ask that Paraweena, gov. You ask, boyo. You do that...

   (They return to the circle.

   The rhythm sticks calm down)

MELLIN: I lost my temper. That old man was sitting there so heavily, and I know he wasn't believing me.

MRS MELLIN: Ssh, James, ssh. You're trying too hard. Just remember they're only paying you at the probationary rate.

MELLIN: You go on back in. I'll try to find out why they're so agitated tonight.

MRS MELLIN: If you're set on it, James, I can't stop you. Just be careful. They must be near animals when they howl like this.

   (Background noise and rhythm build up as the MELLINS return to the circle. Then silence. Actors move to places for next scene)

Scene 3

   (Scene played in silence, low key. All actors seated and very little movement)

TRUGANINNI: Paraweena is going. Why should I not go too.

GUDJARA: Where is your sister?

MANGANA: (fatally) Gone. Gone.

GUDJARA: Your father has said no, Truganinni. You should see why.

TRUGANINNI: But I am to go with Paraweena. Is that different from being followed by you? He is your son; he will be my husband.

GUDJARA: Questions!

TRUGANINNI: He is your son, and it will not take long. Across the water with the wood, then we are back here again. That white man from the hut, he asked Paraweena about it. He knows. What is wrong. Father!
   (pause)
I have not seen over there. If you look in the morning, it comes out of the mist. If you look in the evening, the ripples come from there. You have seen me looking, Gudjara.

GUDJARA: (irritably) Yes, yes.

TRUGANINNI: You see? Father? The white fellow is there, but Paraweena is strong. I shall look from behind him.

MANGANA: No.

   (TRUGANINNI stamps her foot, then threatens GUDJARA)

TRUGANINNI: Tomorrow, I will run across the mountains and you will have to follow.

GUDJARA: I would catch you, then use a stick.

TRUGANINNI: (shrewdly) But if I go with those men and Paraweena, and you come too. It is not as far as the mountains.

   (Pause)

GUDJARA: (To MANGANA,) I would rather go with my son, old friend.

   (Pause. MANGANA looks up slowly and nods.

Clap of rhythm sticks.

Delighted, TRUGANINNI runs back to the circle. The old man follows her as quickly as he can.

Blackout)

Scene 4

(Rhythm builds up, stops suddenly.

Late afternoon light circles MANGANA.

MELLIN rises, moves central hesitatingly)

MRS MELLIN: It's no good interfering.

MELLIN: Look at him.

MRS MELLIN: James, you can't understand their ways. They've not been used to anything else. It's in their nature.

MELLIN: If I can, I'll help him.

MRS MELLIN: You can see he doesn't want to know, James.

MELLIN: (sadly) I don't know what I see.

MRS MELLIN: There's no sense in talking to you. I'm going back, James. It's coming on to rain.

(MELLIN advances. MRS MELLIN retires, but does not leave the stage)

MELLIN: Mangana, though you won't look at me, I've something to say.
    (pause)
I'm... sorry, old man.

MRS MELLIN: (shocked) James!

MELLIN: (snaps at her) I said I was sorry!
   (then)
Go on back.
   (turns again to MANGANA)
Last night your people were mourning. It was for your daughter Jalmarida, wasn't it?
   (at the name, MANGANA looks up at him)
It was for Jalmarida, wasn't it?

MANGANA: What do you want?

MELLIN: (with signs) Jalmarida - won't - be - coming - back.

(MANGANA understands the 'sense', turns away)

MELLIN: I told you. I didn't know it was her. You didn't understand.

MRS MELLIN: James, it's all falling on deaf ears. Come away.

MELLIN: BE QUIET!

(Silence. Then rhythm builds up)

MANGANA: Now, all but one, my family is gone. I am left with Truganinni and a life I remember. My foolish Truganinni, will you cry for your sister now? I am your father and I want you here now. Darkness comes; you should be here with your father now. We should weep for your sister together. Now your sister comes back no more. A darkness comes. You should be here...
   (then particularly startled)
Truganinni? Truganinni?
   (controls himself)
You are with Gudjara. Gudjara is with you; you have him bring you back now. We should weep together and your father is old...

MRS MELLIN: James, I need to light the lanterns. Look at the sky.

MANGANA: I look at the sky. Black, black. Soon I will see nothing more. When the sun dies so too will Mangana. My daughter has not come back and the sun is dying. Mangana will not see and Truganinni should be waiting. Truganinni should be waiting...

CHORUS:
Ss! Ss! The wind, the sky,
The dark, the night, the moon
The moon is not rising.
Where is Gudjara?
The girl, the young man are still with him;
Truganinni still wanders.
Where now is the old man?
The light dies to be born
The star lizard swims into night
They should return
They should return
We search with our hearts
We are looking with, our eyes
And Mangana is waiting
Ss! Ss! The wind, the sky,
The dark, the night, the moon gone
And Truganinni still wanders.

(In sudden silence again)

MANGANA: Across the air, I heard a scream! Gudjara, Gudjara, you do not return! Do not stay any longer there; our people now sing. The night brings the whisper. Listen from here. Bring back my daughter!

CHORUS:
Truganinni still wanders.
Where now is the old man?
The light dies to be born
The star lizard swims into dark
The moon has wandered
We are looking with our eyes
And Mangana is waiting.

(Urgent rhythm-stick beating)

MANGANA: Gudjara, bring Truganinni!

MELLIN: (at MANGANA) What is it?

MANGANA: BRING BACK MY DAUGHTER!

(Nothing. He rocks with grief)

MRS MELLIN: Don't try to understand this one, James. You will meddle. Has he appreciated it? Has he tried?

MELLIN: There's something more.

MRS MELLIN: (scared) What more could there be? Leave him, for God's sake. Look how dark it's getting suddenly. If he wants something let him go to the proper authorities.

MELLIN: I am the proper authority, woman! Leave us alone for a while.

MRS MELLIN: I can't go back alone. I'm scared, James.'

(MANGANA looks up suddenly. He has heard something. He gets to his feet, peers into distance)

MELLIN: (to her) Wait!

(The three stay silent, waiting. A long pause)

MANGANA: Truganinni...?
    (then)
Truganinni...?

(TRUGANINNI walks slowly and painfully back into the clearing. She keeps her head turned away from her father. When she finally does break the heavy silence, it is in monotone, degraded, introjected)

TRUGANINNI: Father, Paraweena has not come back with me. My Paraweena, he has not come back. Gudjara has not come back with me, Father.

MANGANA : (outcry) *Tell me!*

(All actors freeze, look straight out at TRUGANINNI; essential, economical reaction only.

With abject shame, she keeps her head turned from MANGANA as she speaks and as she slowly sinks down at his feet)

TRUGANINNI: We were... on the water. Those two men had not spoken to us, but they smiled at me. They had smiled at me and were bringing us home. Gudjara fell asleep, the old man was tired. Paraweena held my arm. He... screamed for me when they pushed him over. Gudjara jumped up but one of them hit him. The other slapped me and pushed me down. I saw Gudjara's head as he tried to get back in. Paraweena was calling but I could not get up. I could see their hands. One of those men shouted and picked up an axe. He chopped off their hands as they clung to the side. He... chopped off their hands as they clung to the side, Father. I saw them drown and their hands float away.
   (cringes from MANGANA's attempt to touch her arm)
One of those men was laughing. Whenever he could, he would reach down and touch me. They pulled me to where they wanted to go. My legs were not strong enough to keep them away, Father. Why should that be? I am Mangana's daughter They would not let me turn my head away.
   (then terribly simply:)
They... hit me, father, at both my ends.

(MANGANA drops his head in utter hopelessness)

MELLIN goes up to TRUGANINNI)

MELLIN: What is it, girlie?

(He has broken the stillness of their grief with this.

MANGANA loses control)

MANGANA: Aah... !

(MANGANA leaps onto MELLIN from behind and begins to strangle him. MELLIN is helpless. MRS MELLIN screams, fumbles in her bag. She pulls out an old pistol, aims blindly and fires. MANGANA falls.

MELLIN rolls from out under. MRS MELLIN becomes hysterical. TRUGANINNI looks at her father and does so without comprehension of any of this)

MRS MELLIN: (hysterically) I told you. I told you. He was killing you. He was going to kill you!. Oh, why wouldn't you listen?!

(MELLIN walks slowly over to her, leads her out.

TRUGANINNI crawls over to MANGANA, kneels beside him.

The actors freeze in position)

<u>Blackout</u>)

Part 2: Pantagruel In-between

George Augustus Robinson was the most successful of the 'conciliators' of the 1830s who went out into the bush to 'round up' the Tasmanians peacefully. (Alexander McKay of Part 3 was also one of them.) Robinson went on to be the guiding light of the 'out of sight, out of mind' policy and of the school which was set up for the Tasmanians' so-called education on Flinders Island in Bass Strait. He administered the establishment with (some say) great cruelty. Or was it stupidity? Or was it misguided pity? And along strict catechistic lines. (The question-and-answer scene in this play is authentic as to its setting and catechistic zeal.)

The Tasmanians died one by one, just as much through morbid longing for their homeland as any obvious clinical cause.

Later, Robinson was appointed Chief Protector of Aboriginals (Australian) of the Port Phillip District in what was to become Melbourne and its environs.

He was allowed to take five Tasmanians (one of them Truganinni) with him as servants. But he seemed to care little for them. They wandered as far as South Australia; they argued with, and killed, a white man; and the two men were hanged. They had the dubious honour of being the first Australian tribal people ever to be so. Truganinni, perhaps as a woman, was acquitted. But, even here, she witnessed a horrible deaths of her fellow Tasmanians... perhaps equally as devastating to her as witnessing the postmortem butchery of King Billy. On the first hanging attempt, the gallows trap wouldn't open. On the second attempt, one of the men tumbled and was killed instantly; the other's noose slipped out of place and he suffered an agonizing death. Jack Ketch the hangman got £10 for his 'expertise' at the job.

Part 2: List of Characters

ROBINSON, Chief Protector of Aboriginals
DOVE, his assistant
TRUGANINNI
BOB, Tasmanian
MRS CLARK, a catechist on the Flinders Island 'camp'
1ST GOVERNMENT INSPECTOR
2ND GOVERNMENT INSPECTOR
BOY, young Tasmanian
ACHILLES, elderly Tasmanian
APHRODITE, elderly Tasmanian

Scene 1

(The scene is set as though it is another half of the set from Part 1 which itself has been slid off half the stage. The alfresco setting is divided from the living-room setting of Play 3 by a curtain or some other similar prop that makes no pretensions to be anything other than an artificial barrier.

Though the stage thus looks incongruous, no attempt should be made to ameliorate this impression. Indeed, it must be as theatrical as George Augustus Robinson is theatrical; it must 'fit' him feeling quite at home in his self-satisfaction if not downright pomposity.

Note: In the directions of this play, the division (whether it be a curtain, a piece of material, a step dividing different levels, a 'wall and door' etc) will be referred to as the 'curtain' for simplicity.

On the living room side, GEORGE AUGUSTUS ROBINSON is slouched at a desk. He picks his nose and, sure that no one is watching, chews on the pickings. He scratches with relish. Other than these, there is no movement positively until someone in the audience makes a noise. ([Somebody will sooner or later.) At this, ROBINSON starts and, by reflex action, adjusts his whole bearing into a more 'proper' pose. Thus collected, thus suited for being 'public', he smiles at nothing in particular. It is an awkward smile, managing to convey more fawning than pleasure. Then he gets to his feet, rounds on a wall mirror and bows, preens before it)

ROBINSON: George Augustus Robinson.

(DOVE appears. He is put out, still buttoning his coat. He stands formally at the rear of the living room)

DOVE: ...Esquire. Pacificator and...

(ROBINSON claps his hands. DOVE stops. It shows he is quite mindless of DOVE.)

ROBINSON: (carrying on introducing himself) And my assistant Dove. In my position here...

DOVE: (piping up) ...Chief Protector of Aborigines, by appointment of HRH Queen Victoria, by recommendation of the Prime Minister, the English Prime Minister, through the Home Secretary for approval and the Governor for endorsement, through trickle-trickle clerks and councils and lesser leagues, the commission thereby and duly signed...

ROBINSON: (demurely, again) In my...

DOVE: ...by Royal Seal.

ROBINSON: (above him) In my position here, I need an assistant. But the thing is: do I need Dove? Oh, and I am here with various... sundry... characters out back. Behind here, that is, not the... er, Outback, meaning Interior.
   (pause, while he assures himself he is happy with the image put across)
Good. Passably.

(He waves DOVE away with an offhand gesture. When DOVE has gone, he gets on his knees. He does this as not a fit man despite his appearance.

He is front stage, as near to the audience as possible, but the mirror is still his focus)

ROBINSON: Song of praise, spoken, in humble reminder, Your Excellency or whoever you are, that there's only ever been one Chief Protector of Aboriginals. Ever. And I'm it.
   (fanfare, which he acknowledges demurely)
A fine fanfare. A good fanfare. A worthy fanfare. Twas first delivered by my wards after the first whale-boat mail after last Christmas...
   ('praying')

Dear, good God Who Cometh Good for some of us, I know... your some-of-us attempt things that others would not. This is true. Nevertheless and all the same, it is a sobering and wonderful thought that I, me, whichever, George Augustus Robinson, sometime boot-maker that I was, has been lifted from the last, metaphorically speaking ha ha, foisted to the first, winched up by Your Divine Derrick. That I...

> *(Re-enter DOVE. Stops when he sees ROBINSON, just as ROBINSON has stopped by DOVE's interruption.)*

ROBINSON: You get any of that down, Dove?

DOVE: I knocked, sir reverend sir. The door was shut, so I didn't think you were in, sir. Or out. Or both or either, sir reverend.

ROBINSON: Dove, you are a bumbling fellow. You just saw me here.

DOVE: I did, I did, sir. But I can never believe my eyes seeing you, an' that's the truth of it.

ROBINSON: (smug) Well, well.

> *(DOVE goes to retreat)*

ROBINSON: Dove!

DOVE: (ducking, then realizing error) Sir reverend sir?

ROBINSON: There comes a time, Dove, when a man must face himself. Life is like that, my good fellow, although I can't be too sure about yours. The thing being, Dove... one day you suddenly stumble. You look down. You see your boots. And that is the time you must ask yourself questions, Dove. Do you get my meaning?

DOVE: I assure you I knocked, sir.

ROBINSON: Doubts, Dove.

DOVE: (appalled) Not Dove doubts, sir?

ROBINSON: My doubts have arisen, Dove. Doubts standing before you.

(DOVE hesitates uncomprehendingly. ROBINSON waits for the penny to drop impatiently, before:)

ROBINSON: Remember this, Dove.... It is all in the mirrors.

DOVE: What is, Sir reverend sir?

ROBINSON: The smoke, man, the smoke.

DOVE: Did I light something where I shouldn've, Sir?
(to the other's annoyed click of the tongue)
I really do assure you I had no idea you were in or out or I wouldn't have gone around lighting fires, Sir reverend sir.

(ROBINSON turns away in exasperation. Dove is now totally confused)

DOVE: (sotto voce to off) Did I fluff a cue?

ROBINSON: (heavily, re-prompting) Doubts, Dove, doubts. Have arisen.

DOVE: (tentative) Doubts about your achievements, Sir reverend sit?

ROBINSON: (on the track again) Ah, yes, questions, questions! Self-doubts run a tortuous course, Dove.
    (pause, then prompts)
Yes, you may respond. Broadly will do.

DOVE: Pacificator and...
    (thinks)
Haven't we just been through all this, Sir reverend sir?

ROBINSON: Broadly, broadly. As slow as you like.

(From here on, verbal heralding of rehearsed lines)

DOVE: Pacificator and Conciliator of the species Tasmanoid, the Van Diemens Land Aboriginals.

ROBINSON: (nodding) And today is...

DOVE: Today is the 8th, at the end of November, 1841, being the tenth anniversary of your most successful campaign. Upon which hung a certain tribe's salvation, Sir reverend sir.

ROBINSON: (coolly) Some have viewed it like that.

DOVE: A *whole* race's salvation.

ROBINSON: More have viewed it like that, yes. On a quiet night, one can't help thinking and savouring. And...?

DOVE: And never before had such a white man reached out such a hand to such wild men. Man to savage.

ROBINSON: (self-depreciating) Not exactly savages.

DOVE: Savages comparative.

ROBINSON: Well, well. Natural divisions.

DOVE: Oh Sir reverend sir, though my collar might not fit, my ears haven't been muffled!

ROBINSON: (demurely) I had some help, let's not forget that.
  (homily to mirror)
You may make the shoes, but not the leather. Were you not a mirror, I can be quoted.

DOVE: (going on) Just a black guide or two, that's all.

ROBINSON: For the sake of absolute necessity, mind.

> *(He turns away, sits as The Thinker, causing DOVE to query again his lines. He hisses at 'off')*

DOVE: *Are we still with the mirror?*

ROBINSON: (hearing it) Of course we are.

DOVE: (and so carries on declaring) How you went out to save them when most cried folly, let them die off. All those dark days with those nights coming on. You alone with the stealthy bush and who-knows-what creepy crawlies... the strange howlings at night, knowing the primitives lurked somewhere around probably watching you from the country equivalent of dark comers and blood-red rings around the moon. Alone. With none save thyself, Sir reverend sir. Solitary...

ROBINSON: Incontestably.

DOVE: ...trusting in one God, trustworthy and questionably friendly, and two blacks, friendly and questionably trustworthy...

(TRUGANINNI and BOB enter wearily on the 'bush' side and set up camp.

DOVE watches them as he carries on...)

DOVE: Truganinni and Bob. Your only companions. As such.

ROBINSON: Aye, 'as such'. Still, I considered them as people, nonetheless.
 (sighs world wearily. To audience and to mirror)
Excuse me.

(He manages to raise himself, moves through 'curtain' dividing the sets, gets tangled up. Manages to extricate himself, then immediately feigns the extreme exhaustion of a long trek as he crosses to TRUGANINNI and BOB. He flops down)

ROBINSON: It's no good, my friends. They'll just have to come to me. I can no longer pretend that I'm tired, because I am. And to think this morning we were gaining on them. Now here we are, back where we started this morning. All in all, six complete circles I'd say. It's making me sweat.
 (sniffs)

I need a change.
    (accusingly at them)
Or is it one of you? If it is, I rely on you removing yourself.

(They don't answer)

ROBINSON: How many would you say are there out there this time?

BOB: Lot.

ROBINSON: (despondent) I thought we had the remainder of the whole tribe this morning.

TRUGANINNI: They will come.

ROBINSON: (shaking his head) Five days is too much.

TRUGANINNI: Now they will come. They could not while we followed. It is the custom.

ROBINSON: (sulkily) You could have said, Truganinni.

TRUGANINNI: They are too tired keeping ahead of us. One of the women, she told me.

ROBINSON: (reacting) One of the women told you?

TRUGANINNI: They are my friends, but I do not like them.

ROBINSON: But I've been chasing them for days, woman!
    (but then enthusiastic)
You've told them about my offer, then?

TRUGANINNI: (shrugging) Forgot.

ROBINSON: You couldn't have!

TRUGANINNI: They are bad fellows, these.

ROBINSON: Truganinni, Truganinni, you speak to them.

TRUGANINNI: You go.

ROBINSON: You don't have to be embarrassed by the way they dress... don't dress... like I have to.
   (pushing her)
You talk to them.

TRUGANINNI: They will come.

   (She helps BOB with the fire. ROBINSON chuckles.

   As he speaks, the shadows of the 'wild' Tasmanians he is trying to 'conciliate' gradually spread across him)

ROBINSON: The Oyster Bay tribe. Looking like they just come in for a look-see. Walking casually through Hobart Town with them at my side. Hello, Governor. These? Just a few once-hostile family groups I met on the way to tea on   the lawn. Easy to tame. Well, Governor, if you don't mind the fact that you're the one who outlawed them, I'm sure they'd be delighted. Cream and one lump all round can't hurt once. Look how outside the inn they cavort and dance and sing and throw spears. Wonderful, isn't it, nature? They're going to love the school you've built for them. Won't we, lads? ... the pearls of the Oyster Bay tribe.
   (giggles)
The pearls of the Oyster. Put that lot of thirty-five in your ledger next to my name, and pamp it down and smoke it.

   (TRUGANINNI has now stood up, draws his attention to the shadows.

   Seeing them so near, ROBINSON leaps to his feet; dangerous silence)

ROBINSON: (to her, accusingly) You said they were tired. You said.

TRUGANINNI: (simply) They are looking at you.

ROBINSON: (shrinking) Do you think they can see me?

(Menacing silence until it is relieved when DOVE simply put his head through the curtain divide and ...)

DOVE: (from 'living-room' side) Your track and the savages, Sir reverend sir...

(ROBINSON pats 'excuse me' on TRUGANINNI's shoulder and briskly moves back through the dividing curtain, this time without getting too entangled.

TRUGANINNI and BOB freeze.

ROBINSON 'stations' himself chez lui as before)

ROBINSON: As our tracks came together with a lustful joining, so did their lives join destiny with mine.

DOVE: Their first white words. They should have understood them. I would have tried to, Sir.

ROBINSON: (nodding; then evangelically to imaginary Tasmanians) I bring you a message from your brotherly white father you may call Governor or Gov at a pinch. He has told me to tell you he thinks of you more as first cousins than subjects. It is hard, he has told me, to list an official return about you when you make him shoot you with only half the certainty. For that numbers have to be stabilized, he said. He promises you protection, a good place to live, plenty of food, warm coverings for your genitals in particular you will be glad to hear. He wants to protect you and those genitals. He wants to invite you home. He says he would like to have you to tea in his big house, the one with the most interesting topiarized tea-trees south of the Cape of Good Hope. So, come, come. Your sins are forgiven, some even forgotten. Follow in my footsteps and learn to walk with God!
   (pause for afflatus to subside, then nods end-game to DOVE) So, Dove, there is your mirror and there is your smoke. I recommend it to be remembered.

(He returns to TRUGANINNI and BOB, takes up former position of fearful apprehension. And quakes in the

direction of the shadows of the 'wild' Tasmanian tribespeople)

ROBINSON: I bring you a message from your brotherly white father. He has told me to tell you he thinks of you more as first cousins than subjects. It is...
  (into air)
Etcetera, etcetera.
  (then musters up)
Come! Come!

TRUGANINNI: (pointing out the fact) They have come. And gone.

ROBINSON: Where?

TRUGANINNI: (shrugs) Places around.

ROBINSON: What, then?

TRUGANINNI: Bad fellows, these.

(Chanting and rhythm sticks begins off)

ROBINSON: (fearful again) What's going on?

TRUGANINNI: They are jumping around.

ROBINSON: (agitated) It's getting dark.

(They settle. When they have done so, ROBINSON gets up, hurries into 'living-room' side and resumes declarations to mirror, to audience as though continuing public speaking)

ROBINSON: There were nights when I could not be sure of seeing the dawn again. Such a night was that one. Try though I might, I could not get to sleep. Next morning, because of it all, I'm afraid my edge was somewhat dampened. And I overslept. But, even with that, I still could not bring myself to curse the day they were born.

(He quickly returns to 'bush' set, lies down in sleep again with woollen cap.

Quick and theatrical dawn.

Shadows, obviously with spears, fall across the group. TRUGANINNI springs up)

TRUGANINNI: (eventually defiantly) What are those spears for?

ROBINSON: What's that one saying?

TRUGANINNI: He says, not right to kill you like this with that thing on your head.

ROBINSON: And?

TRUGANINNI: (laconically) Others say who cares.

ROBINSON: More, more. He is answering.

TRUGANINNI: He says best you undress first.

ROBINSON: (outraged) What? Take up the cloth?

(The spears are raised. At this, TRUGANINNI and BOB bolt, leaving ROBINSON to be enveloped by shadows)

ROBINSON: What do you want? Eh? Eh? You want me to meet my Maker as naked as the day I left Him? Look, one day you'll be reasonable people. I wouldn't use force to stop you… being reasonable.
    (stops confused by himself)
That's not my nature, you see. If you really have to leave, please don't feel wildly free. Or…
    (weak laugh)
freely wild. I give you my word as a man of … OH, GOD!

(He bolts too. As he does so, and thankfully for him, BOB springs back into the clearing as a decoy)

BOB: Ay! Ay!

(All freeze.

As quickly as is possible, ROBINSON dives on stage from the wings on the opposite 'living-room' side. Pauses to gather his breath, before...)

ROBINSON: I could only be thankful to my Maker that, in his panic, Bob had stumbled back into the very clearing he had bolted from. It was a fortuitous diversion. I ran, of course. Any one of you who has had to hop it through the Van Diemens Land bush with wildmen pounding along behind will know what it's like to... to be chased by blacks through the Van Diemens Land bush with wildmen pounding behind. Anyway, all I could do was to break more wind and leave what was left to Providence.

(ROBINSON exits. As immediately as possible, he re-appears -- backwards and crouched --from wings on the 'bush' side.

At the same time, TRUGANINNI enters in the same manner upstage.

They creep in parabolically until they theatrically back into each other)

ROBINSON: Aagh! (recognising her, casting about wildly) Where, where?

TRUGANINNI: (matter-of-factly) They have killed him, I think.

ROBINSON: Who?

TRUGANINNI: The other. That Bob who saved you.

ROBINSON: I don't want them to have to answer to God on account of me!

(TRUGANINNI shrugs. ROBINSON notices the river)

ROBINSON: The river. Truganinni!. Our main camp over there! Our soup's up here!

TRUGANINNI: The river, yes.

ROBINSON: It's flowing swiftly. We'll have to be sharp. Keep up, woman, and I'll see you safe yet...!

> *(Grabs her arm, goes to dash off. But stops when DOVE, from the 'living-room' side, speaks...)*

DOVE: And so they did.

ROBINSON: (prompts across 'divide') Yes, yes, and what...?

DOVE: Did follow you to salvation. More than a gross of them.

> *(ROBINSON let her arm fall. He walks, puffed, to front of stage)*

ROBINSON: Much nearer two, Dove.

DOVE: They did by the hundreds. You saved a whole nation.

ROBINSON: Noble fellows all. I remember a number of them quite distinctly. Matter of fact, I believe there's still quite a number of them left.

> *(theatrical pause, then turns back to TRUGANINNI, takes her by the arm again, then resumes position of midflight.')*

ROBINSON: Keep up, my good woman, and I'll save you yet...!

(and dashes off with her, but stops a second time after a few paces. Incredulous, dawning pause)

ROBINSON: I can't swim... You know I can't swim. Truganinni!
    (she shrugs what-to-do)
The raft! Where is it?

TRUGANINNI: (pointing across river) Across there.

ROBINSON: Then how did we get here?

TRUGANINNI: I and Bob carried you. Anyway, they have seen it. Some will be waiting for you with smiles on their faces.

ROBINSON: The cunning black bastards!

(Realising this mistake he quickly turns back to front stage and, either to mirror on other side or to the audience, recants:)

ROBINSON: You understand I was under considerable strain.

(He waits until he hears no objections, then nods got-away-with-that and turns back to TRUGANINNI, but DOVE's voice stops him before he can resume flight)

DOVE: It can't be true about those two, sir!

ROBINSON: (suspiciously) Which two?

DOVE: Those two guides, Truganinni and Bob. You can't owe your life to them on a number of occasions, Sir reverend sir, the word going around.

ROBINSON: Don't be a complete duffer, Dove. There's slander abroad, mind, my lad.

DOVE: Oh infamy, sir...

ROBINSON: And men who make them. Men who make them. What do you yourself think?

DOVE: Some fool did assure me, Sir reverend sir.

ROBINSON: Pure flights of fancy. Some agnostic fantasy. Can God's work be done by spear-throwers, lad? I mean, *think*.

DOVE: Heaven forbid, Sir reverend sir.

ROBINSON: Well.

(Satisfied he has countered that, he moves into the living-room side and presents himself)

ROBINSON: Speech to the Parramatta Party for Preserving Preventions, New South Wales, late 30's. Despite minor heckling...
    ('delivering')
That one called Truganinni if I remember... she informed me, under such trepidation that I had to knock it out of her, that they had killed the other native. In the circumstances, this proved untrue, but wholly understandable. She then rather pathetically urged me to hide in the bushes nearby. I explained to her the inadvisability of that course for the moment, whereupon I explored the possibility of broaching the river across which either she or the native Bob had so carelessly left it. Finally, after repeated attempts to manage both the camouflaged tree trunk fashioned out of my own hand and the woman's hysteria, I reached the safety of the other bank whenceupon I then proceeded to my main encampment.
    (pause)
I had brought the native woman along through all this, rather careless if I may say to my own safety. Her name was -- perhaps still is, although they chop-and-change so -- Truganinni. It was interesting to note the woman's subsequent devotion to me, and probably quite justified.

(Pause for a lacklustre applause by DOVE. Then ROBINSON returns to TRUGANINNI and assumes flight position with her)

ROBINSON: Over *there*? My God, Truganinni, that means the raft's out when it should be *in*!

TRUGANINNI: There is a tree down over there. It will float with you if I pull it after me.

ROBINSON: Truganinni, dear, dear woman, long-time companion, for the love of God, try!
    (dashes off to hide)
Call me when you're ready!

> (stops on thought)

But not too loud with the calling!

> *(TRUGANINNI follows him out, walking. Blackout on 'bush' side.*
>
> *ROBINSON re-enters on 'living-room' side, catches breath by flopping into chair at desk. Then assumes academic pose with letter in hand.)*

ROBINSON: Correspondence to a friend in...

> *(stops for a long 'unrehearsed' pause. Whispering and then prompts from wings and DOVE. After a while, ROBINSON tries again)*

ROBINSON: Correspondence to a friend in...
> (Stops, irritated)

It's no good, you know.

DOVE: (psst) Sir!

ROBINSON: (annoyed) It's no good. Something's very wrong. Today...
> (clicking fingers)...

today...

DOVE: (emerging) Today is the 8th, sometime in November, eighteen forty...

ROBINSON: I know that.

DOVE: ... one. The tenth anniversary of your most successful campaign. Upon which hung...
> (stops)

I definitely know we've been through this bit.

ROBINSON: (out of character) Oh, keep it own, will you?

DOVE: (down from his 'role') You packing it in then?

ROBINSON: Listen, Dove or whatever your name is, there's something else today. A man doesn't stand around boot to boggle without something-being-very- wrong deep down. I don't know if it's something I forgot before that bloody bus was late getting me here, or it's something you'n'I have buggered up. It's got to be you when I think of it. I can't think of anybody I'd doubt less than me.

DOVE: Fair go.

ROBINSON: Something ain't right, I tell you.

DOVE: You get a touch of stage fright, like?

ROBINSON: I tell you something's not right. What about the fumbling, bumbling start. You made.

DOVE: Me?

ROBINSON: The lines you fluffed. Me feeling stared at being caught in that curtain thing there. Listen, caught picking my nose! Don't think I don't know that.

DOVE: (patting his shoulder) Don't take it so hard.

ROBINSON: Get your hands off me! There. Even you. Give you an inch and you take a mile.

DOVE: (coy) You didn't say that last night.

ROBINSON: I was trying to forget... something... last night.

DOVE: Go on, it's probably only the trial.

ROBINSON: (reacting) The trial!

DOVE: It's probably that.. Your Truganinni-not doing what she was told, and all.

ROBINSON: By God, that's it! Bloody hell, what treachery! No wonder I couldn't sleep.

DOVE: Take it easy.

ROBINSON: It's all right for you. I've got responsibility, a position. Oh, why did they have to go and kill some... some white trash on some trashy open road where everybody could see because that's what they're always looking for, trash.

DOVE: There you go.. Can I go back to Sir reverend sir again?

ROBISON: What could I do about it? I didn't even know they'd got out through the bars, let alone been gone a week.

DOVE: It was atrocious behaviour, Sir reverend sit!

ROBINSON: Too right it was. I told 'em, I said, no atrocious behaviour while you're my wards in this house. This is Melbourne now, I said, not your Hobart Town. And you tell me, Dove, what's more atrocious than breaking out and all five of them, walking overland to Adelaide.

DOVE: Atrocious... them walking or Adelaide, sir?

ROBINSON: Adelaide, of course. And nearly getting there. If they hadn't killed that white trash... and I do wish you wouldn't keep calling him that, Dove... if they had made it to Adelaide, Dove, can you imagine Adelaide being more worse for wear?

DOVE: Shudder, sir!

ROBINSON: After all I've done for them. Bringing them to Melbourne, letting them share the glory of my promotion. Allotting my own servants' quarters to them. There's right and there's wrong, man; you yourself have heard me personally getting them to repeat that in English, Dove.

DOVE: I have, indeedee,

ROBINSON: And damn it, murder is wrong!

DOVE: It is, Sir reverend sir.

ROBINSON: They could have asked you that. You would have known that. The years I've spent in trying to get them to speak properly. The Robinson stress on the adverbial and all that, if I may say so m'self. The father I've been.

DOVE: Mustn't upset yourself, sir.

ROBINSON: (hotly) Father, I say! When I could have been fathering elsewhere!

DOVE: Ssh, sir, you'll need the sleep tonight.

ROBINSON: Only last week, that Truganinni stood right there where you are, Dove, and said, pitiably, 'You be Father; I'll pour'. And now this. Some Yankee whaler killed, some ordinary little judge holding a public trial, and my name dragged through the mud. I'll wager that. My sacrifices will mean nothing. Instead, I will have to stand by and watch while the fruits of my labour drop, plop.

DOVE: Not plop?

ROBINSON: Yes. Splat plop. Gallows, you know.

DOVE: Poor unfortunates.

ROBINSON: Murderers, murderers. Let's not mince words. From my voluntarily-given protection, my own house. Truganinni, that one. That Bob. Jack. Yes. Matilda. ...what's the other's name?

DOVE: I don't think you'd quite gotten around to giving him a name, Sir.

ROBINSON: . Harried, harried, Dove.
    (then tedious decision)
You'd better go.

DOVE: Beg yours?

ROBINSON: You'd better attend the trial. Call me when I'm expected in court but delay it so I can't possible make it.

DOVE: (indicating stage) But I haven't finished a few scenes here yet...

ROBINSON: I can manage on my own. Underlie any bits you think important.

(DOVE is confused, hesitates)

ROBINSON: Go on, I say.

DOVE: Oh, why is it always me.

(and huffs off in irritation.

Long pause. Finally ROBINSON goes wearily back to the desk, sits, picks up the letter again)

ROBINSON: (tries again) Correspondence to a friend in...

(DOVE pops his head back in)

DOVE: The letter. Are you sure you can manage?

(ROBINSON waves him roughly away, re-arranges himself)

ROBINSON: Correspondence to a friend via a letter, care of Oswaldtwistle Presbytery, Sussex, England. Authenticated as being my hand writing when Superintendent of the camp on Flinders Island for additional remnants in Bass Strait running with Antipodean undercurrents...

(As he reads, lighting on 'bush' side of set, where MRS CLARK mimes teaching, preaching, beseeching and singing of prayers, and the 1ST and 2ND GOVERNMENT INSPECTORS mime officialdom)

ROBINSON: 'Well. Floriana, History does not furnish another instance where a whole race has been treated to so humane a policy of conciliation and protection.'
    (to mirror)
Let those in court answer that.

(back to letter)
'After I and others...
   (adds in correction)
a *few* others... had gathered these piteous primitives like wild flowers to the bosom of God, we had them repatriated to this school. Ah, and what a singular establishment it is! Nowhere else could Stone Age bodily functions come to express perfectly Christian prayer. A one Mrs Clark and I have to carry the burden. Even so, we furl and unfurl did a-furling go the Union Jack each and furl and unfurl did a-furling go every sunset and sunrise. Sabbath day observation and no moving around; nightly prayers at six and eight. No unsupervised dancing allowed and even then only in neck-to-knee garments. Latin inscriptions, not just your ordinary catechisms. But I won't go on. After thousands of years in the dark, you can imagine how they take it. Even now we are all eagerly preparing for the annual Government inspection...'

(At this stage, MRS CLARK and the INSPECTORS are waiting formally for him. They look mutely in his direction. He puts the letter down)

ROBINSON: (finalises reading) 'I'll carry on with this later, dear Floriana.'
   (gets up and moves over to her side)
Right, Mrs Clark, if the Inspectors are ready, let us proceed.

MRS CLARK: (nods, but hesitated) Er...?

ROBINSON: (patiently) Call in the advanced class please, Mrs Clark.

(She titters out. He turns to THE INSPECTORS)

ROBINSON: Gentlemen, this won't take long. When they know we're ready for them, you can't imagine the excited state they get into. They'll positively stampede in.
   (waits. Fills in with:)
They've been waiting six months for this. Some of them get so wound up they want to know what six months is.
   (waits, but still nothing)

You'll see yourself how proud they are. Indeed, we are all proud! I and my staff are certainly bulging chests have. I trust that you too will leave here feeling that there's something worth saving in these sad, sad creatures.

(calls)

Mrs Clark?

(nothing)

Poor Mrs Clark, can't get around like she used to. Not too sprightly. Hips don't you know.
    (silence now embarrassing and produce verbal burst)
One thing I am certain of, gentlemen. Skin colour, sun-exposed or not, barbarian or British stock, it's not quite the whole story.

(Waits)

2ND INSPECTOR: (not understanding) Quite.

ROBINSON: As you will see. Despite voices raised against us, gentlemen. Many voices.

(Waits)

2ND INSPECTOR: (platitude) A great man proves himself above such rumours, I should have thought, Mr Robinson.

ROBINSON: Precisely, sir.

1ST INSPECTOR: (dislike) You are aware, then, that there are some expressions of doubt about your school here?

ROBINSON: (appeals to mirror) What could that possibly mean? What was meant by that?

(He remains with his circumspection, his back to them, until finally MRS CLARK returns. She has one boy in tow)

ROBINSON: (roughly) The whole class, Mrs Clark.

(MRS CLARK signs to speak with ROBINSON privately.

He goes over in annoyance)

MRS CLARK: (near tears) They can't be found.

ROBINSON: They're just excited. Look around.

MRS CLARK: 'Ere, they're gone. Scarpa'd. We found this one in a vat. The sergeant had to shut him in to keep him there.

ROBINSON: Well, leave the boy here and bring in the women. Quickly. Now what are you shaking your head for, woman?

MRS CLARK: The women, sir...

ROBINSON: Well?

MRS CLARK: They took off before the men did. Then they came back and started washing their clothes.

ROBINSON: Don't be preposterous!

MRS CLARK: The sergeant says they refused to come up at first. Then they changed their minds. In a while, they told him.

ROBINSON: Washing their clothes?
    (light dawning)
But they'll be standing there naked!

MRS CLARK: Not will. Are. As the day they were born, Mr Robinson!

ROBINSON: They wouldn't dare.

MRS CLARK: They did. All the Sergeant says he can do is look on.

ROBINSON: I bet he would.

1ST INSPECTOR: (aloud) Are you inconvenienced by our visit, Mr Robinson?

ROBINSON: (hard smile) Nothing, nothing. One or two overexcited extra backsides, that's all.
   (back to MRS CLARK)
Quickly, woman, the men. Bring back the men.

MRS CLARK: (bursting into tears) Oh, Mr. Robinson...

ROBINSON: Oh, no.

MRS CLARK: Yes. They've run off with the women's clothes!

ROBINSON: Depravity! Depravity all around us!

MRS CLARK: There are one or two stragglers, Mr Robinson.

ROBINSON: Can there possibly be?

MRS CLARK: Taking advantage of the open vat the Sergeant found the boy in.

ROBINSON: Bring them in before they've done with it!

(MRS CLARK rushes out.

ROBINSON recovers to be the genial host again)

ROBINSON: My apologies, gentlemen, it seems the excitement... We don't believe in a lot of discipline.. (darkly) ... as yet.
   (then, brighter)
Take this sturdy young specimen. What's your name, lad?

BOY: Constitution.

ROBINSON: (proudly) Almost first thing, I renamed them all. Though not one of our more advanced, the boy can count...

BOY (too keenly) One... two... three... six.

ROBINSON: ... and slightly add, all at the same time. As I recall, he reads well from the authorized text of 1609, but has been known to stumble on the Revelations. The days of the week and the months are also well within his grasp. What's today, boy?

BOY: Constitution!

ROBINSON: Has slight trouble with oral skills, but attends family worship every evening, arriving in good time. Ah.

(Re-enter MRS CLARK, virtually pushing ACHILLES, the old man; APHRODITE, the old woman; and TRUGANINNI. The Tasmanians are dressed in the most clownish hand-me-downs as though TRUGANINNI has deliberately outfitted them so from the clothing store.

They form a really burlesque-looking group)

MRS CLARK: (introducing) Achilles. Aphrodite. Truganinni.

2ND INSPECTOR: Who?

MRS CLARK: Truganinni, sir.

2ND INSPECTOR: I say, original aboriginal. Which one?
    (pointing to the old woman)
Her?

(The old woman, graced by this attention, stands in a lewd 'femme fatale' pose of come-on at him)

MRS CLARK: That's Aphrodite. That's the Goddess of Love.

(The 2ND INSPECTOR backs off quickly)

ROBINSON: Truganinni's father was Mangana, chief of the Bruni tribe.
    (Intimately)
A princess, locally, but you have to keep a bit of a straight face.. Somewhat obstinate. Most of our women were rescued from captivity amongst the sealers. Think of the depravity. Now, to all

who know, they exhibit virtues formerly reserved only for vicars' wives and governors' ladies. The leather binding of certain parts help there.

2ND INSPECTOR: They certainly look well fed.

MRS CLARK: (whispering) Mr Robinson, I don't think they're going to stay very long.

ROBINSON: Proceed, Mrs C.

MRS CLARK: (confronting the Tasmanians) Now wait for the questions...
  (begins formal catechisms)
Who is God?

BOY: My father!

MRS CLARK: Who was Jesus? Achilles?

ACHILLES: My father.

MRS CLARK: Who is the Reverend Robinson?

APHRODITE: (senilely, but eager) My father, my father...

> *(and continues to chuckle and indicate he and her should get together...)*

MRS CLARK: How can you get to heaven?

ACHILLES: (rushing ahead) Keep clothes on!

MRS CLARK: No Ach...

ACHILLES: Make own bread!

> *(And interrupts MRS CLARK each time she goes to speak with...)*

ACHILLES: Drink tea! No dance, no song! No kill sheep! No bugger-bugger!

BOY: Run away chop-chop!

ROBINSON: Stop interrupting, boy! Go on, Mrs Clark.

MRS CLARK: Have you a soul?

(General puzzlement)

MRS CLARK: Truganinni? Have you a soul?

TRUGANINNI: (irritably) Yes.

MRS CLARK: Will you die?

BOY: (eagerly, hand up) Me!

MRS CLARK: Who crucified Jesus?

(No volunteers)

MRS CLARK: Truganinni?

ROBINSON: (aside) Our brightest pupil...

(But TRUGANINNI still refuses to answer)

MRS CLARK: Who crucified Jesus, Truganinni?

TRUGANINNI: (softly) I hear him scream in the night, longing for home.

2ND INSPECTOR: I say...

1ST INSPECTOR: (to MRS CLARKJ Would you repeat that? What did she mean?

(MRS CLARK looks at TRUGANINNI^ but gets no explanation)

MRS CLARK: I don't think she knows herself, sir.

ROBINSON: (quickly) Go on then, Mrs C.

1ST INSPECTOR: Wait a minute. I want to question this...

> *(ROBINSON jumps between him and TRUGANINNI and conducts them like a choir-master. After each concerted answer, there is a fanfare off, which he acknowledges with the rococo gestures of Commedia dell'arte)*

ROBINSON: Did you know anything of God before you came to this establishment?

BOY: NO!

ACHILLES: NO!

APHRODITE: NO!

ROBINSON: Did you ever pray to God when you lived like savages?

BOY: NO!

ACHILLES: NO!

APHRODITE: NO!

ROBINSON: Were you happy before I taught you about the Lord?

BOY: NO!

ACHILLES: NO!

APHRODITE: NO!

ROBINSON: Are you lost to God's kingdom?

BOY: NO!

ACHILLES: NO! NO!

APHRODITE: NO NO!

ROBINSON: (final flourish) Hurrah the Good News!!

(Final fanfare. ROBINSON sweeps a bow, stands mannered and plumed. After a while, he snaps his fingers in an over-the-shoulder gesture, obviously expecting the INSPECTORS to disappear from his horizon.

He turns and casually walks toward the curtain divide. The 2ND INSPECTOR has to waylay him)

2ND INSPECTOR: Mr Robinson.

(ROBINSON stops)

2ND INSPECTOR: I am frankly worried. I fear my report will look bad, sir.

ROBINSON: I hope there are no grounds for complaint, Mr Inspector?

2ND INSPECTOR: Absolutely not, you understand. I would not have brought the matter up had it not been for this wretched report to be accurate as possible.

ROBINSON: I understand perfectly.

2ND INSPECTOR: It's these blasted returns.

ROBINSON: Trouble?

1ST INSPECTOR: (sarcastically) Just a little matter of a deficit of thirty or so natives since the last return was lodged a year ago.

2ND INSPECTOR: (puzzlement) I've added and re-added. I'm worried about the comment in the margins the matter might draw, you see. Really messify the ledgers, you know. Perhaps if I could just round them off as escapees ...?

(ROBINSON shakes his head sadly)

ROBINSON: That would indicate a certain dissatisfaction amongst the natives, would it now?

2ND INSPECTOR: No deep well around the establishment…?
(ROBINSON shakes his head again)
No natural catastrophe last winter?
(ditto reaction)
Well, what about rounding to the nearest ten whole numbers?

ROBINSON: It is difficult, I agree.

2ND INSPECTOR: It seems so lame to put down 'Inbuilt Obsolescence', that's all.

1ST INSPECTOR: *(confrontation)* On my arrival, Mr Robinson, I found one quarter of them on the sick list. Since then, less than a week, more than a half have been ill in one way or another. This thing, whatever it is, consumption or mental irritant, could wipe out the whole race before long.

ROBINSON: *(self-concerning thought)* It's God's good air, sir. I don't know what you think I can do about it.

1ST INSPECTOR: Have you ever considered a connection between this disease and your attempts to civilize the poor devils?

ROBINSON: Impossible. Why, I myself have had more than a slight cough lately, and look at me. And Mrs Clark here was laid up for two days last week with nasal congestion. Sophistication has nothing to do with it.

1ST INSPECTOR: Need I point out that you have only forty left?

ROBINSON: I realize how some people are talking. Just you remember that when I go to Melbourne to take up my post as Chief Protector of Aborigines ...

2ND INSPECTOR: *(admiringly)* Congratulations, by the way!

ROBINSON: (nodding acknowledgement) ... when I go as the newly-created Protector of Aborigines of the mainland, I am taking five of them with me. Five, sir. Not for my own attendance, either, I may add, but also for their health. Across the Bass Strait, sir! It shows how worried I am.

1ST INSPECTOR: Might you be able to suggest where it will all end?

ROBINSON: Probably not even a thank-you for me.

1ST INSPECTOR: I meant, what do you plan to do about it?

ROBINSON: I shall continue to do all that is humanly possible, adding as I always do 'humane' to that.

2ND INSPECTOR: (Exploding) There's only a bare, miserable forty left, Mr Robinson. For-ty. Four 0.

ROBINSON: I know! I know!

(And escapes across the curtain divide.

Immediately, lights off INSPECTORS.

From the other side, ROBINSON jerks a finger at their going. Feels safe to return and to return to declarations)

ROBINSON: Of course I knew that. Honestly, some people...
    (pause)
The death rate was one frustration, certainly. But I am firmly convinced that my concept would have borne divine fruit had not the mortality rate been so damn high. I mean there are only so many balls one can keep in the air at one time, no?
    (calls)
Dove?
    (no reply)
 Dove?

(DOVE finally puts his head around the door)

DOVE: Be fair, Sir reverend sir. I've only just got back from trying to keep that man's ledger falling out of the boat.

ROBINSON: Did it?

DOVE: Much as I tried, Sir, much as I tried.

ROBINSON: Well, well, let's get on with it.

(And waves him out)

DOVE: All right, all right, I'm going as fast as I can, mate.

(And shuts himself out. ROBINSON thinks of making an issue of DOVE's out-of-character irritability, but thinks better of it, and:)

ROBINSON: ('delivering' again) Of course, I have not been 100 per cent right 100 per cent of the time. But I am content. I have had, by Fate, the Tasmanian Indians... and they in their turn have had it by me. As I have watched over them, I have seen a lot of water pass under the bridge which fell down less than a month after they build it. Let's make it water passing these shores. Oh, yes... currents move while tides ebb and flow. Growth and decay, it's the natural order of things. I may be quoted. Why, even when I...

(Re-enter DOVE without knocking, slams door behind him.)

ROBINSON: Dove! I was meditating.

DOVE: I knocked, didn't I?

ROBINSON: You did not.

DOVE: Knock, knock.

ROBINSON: What's gotten into you, man? You interrupted my train of thought.

DOVE: The door was shut. I didn't think you were in. Or out. Or where you'd gone to.

ROBINSON: Let's not start that again.

DOVE: How do you know I was looking for you, anyway?

ROBINSON: Then who are you looking for?

DOVE: You, of course, 'Sir reverend sir'. That's why I knocked, right?

ROBINSON: I just said you didn't. *You* just said you didn't.

DOVE: Well, the door was shut, so how was I to know someone was behind it in a train of thought?

ROBINSON: It is probably best we are soon parting way, Dove.'

DOVE: Yeah, take five of them but not me.

(disgruntled pause on either side)

ROBINSON: (exasperation) Can we get on?

DOVE: Ask away, 'Sir reverend sir'.

ROBINSON: (back in role) What do you want, lad?

DOVE: I want to apologize for knocking when I didn't think you were in, sir.
   (surly aside)
What the hell else?
   (then)
Oh, and you're being waited on in court.
   (another aside)
Couldn't happen to a nicer bloke.

ROBINSON: (blow-it bombast) The court, the trial! Why is this world so confoundedly cold?

DOVE: (outcry with him) Issue a few more of those nice new blankets you're got in store, for a start.

ROBINSON: The scandal, the smear of it all!
    (and)
Well, Dove, what's the informed opinion?

DOVE: (just to get things right) We've moved on to Melbourne now?

ROBINSON: (with apologetic laugh to mirror or audience of both) We are, Dove, we are. The pitter-patter of it, lad.

DOVE: (back in character) Bob and Jack to hang's the money's on.

ROBINSON: Strong ropes, Dove, strong ropes. I could never keep them on the dangle.
    (and)
What about the females Truganinni and the other, if it was a female.

DOVE: The women acquitted, sir. For humanity's sake. But I've come to tell you, that court there's waiting on you. There's a crowd outside and it's howling your name. So are the accused.

ROBINSON: (pleased) A crowd, you say?

(waving him on)

Well, I'll not shirk my duty, Dove. Chief witness for ... (vaguely) whomsoever.

   (DOVE stops in his tracks)

DOVE: What did you say?

ROBINSON: Chief witness for the whomsoever.

DOVE: (incredulous, not acting) For the defense, not whomsoever. It should be whosoever, anyway.

ROBINSON: What possible defense, Dove?

DOVE: Hey, now listen...

ROBINSON: (over him) I'll be letting the judge know I tried my human best. That's as near as I'm going.

DOVE: (now angry) You're supposed to say for the defense!

ROBINSON: And I'm supposed to be in court too, but I'm not, am I, because you're stopping me.

DOVE: I know the score. You're supposed to send me out to tell the defense lawyer you're coming. I go ahead and you wait here to show them you're not above a bit of playing to the crowd. While you're waiting for the right moment to appear, you stay here and, for sure, you're going to read out the speech you intend to deliver in court.

ROBINSON: Why would I do that?

DOVE: I don't know. How's about to hear your own voice?

ROBINSON: (disgusted) That speech.

DOVE: Yes, that speech.
    (rummages around desk)
This... this... (finds it)...this speech.
    (looking)
Say, you're not fooling are you?

(ROBINSON remains obdurate. DOVE gets angrier)

DOVE: I'm telling you, you're supposed to read...
    (reading from paper)
'Your Eminence Benched so, members of the jury, ladies and gentlemen inside and all those outside straining to hear... yes, I am acquainted, one might say, with the prisoners. As you all know, I have endeavoured to civilize them. I can therefore assure you that they know right from wrong and if that right be my right, then so

be it. I was discussing this very point today with my assistant Dove. Thus it is quite probable that the poor wretches feel guilty about the whole affair of letting down the trust I put in them. I would say more in their defense, but what more can I say, Your High Honour? Thank you, and I say that humbly.'
    (then)
That speech.

ROBINSON: Take it away.

DOVE: (not relenting) At least it was *something*! And then… and then…
    (searches speech again)
…you were supposed to say…

ROBINSON: (mimicking himself) 'Must do everything I can, dear world, everything I can.' Right?

DOVE: Right!

ROBINSON: With heavy irony. Brutal callousness. Yes?

DOVE: Yes!

ROBINSON: And then leave for the trial dripping with a poisonous sneer over my contemptuous arid face...
    (waving vaguely at mirror and audience)
… and they say what a horrible, overblown, nasty little man, before they get up and shake off the peanut shells. Right?

DOVE: No!

ROBINSON: George Augustus Robinson to go out fawning and insufferable. Nothing more than a damn despicable death-dealing dolt as to what appears to public opinion?

DOVE: It's not like that! It's a sense of… I don't know… something!

ROBINSON: Look, Dove or whatever your name is, you don't seem to realize it, but I've got critics. None of your long-haired sufferers with third degree burns looking like tattoos and wigs, but real live critics. They're not going to be satisfied if I come out with a transparent effort like that speech, then cap it with a rotten little drawback of a line like, 'Everything I can, dear world, everything I can' and a sneer. Leave after that? To boos and catcalls? Why should I be jeered off just so everyone can rub their sense of shame on me? I looked after these people; never mind I got a bank balance for the first time in my life. It's my bank balance. I'm the one who's got to sign for it.
    (remembers something around banking)
That reminds me. I have to...

DOVE: (cuts him off) Truganinni and the others are calling out for you, man. Save them!

ROBINSON: I've got the reputation to keep, thank you. One does not keep reputations going into any old court and speaking on behalf of murderers. Or those who thought of doing it. Scriptures, Dove, scriptures.

(DOVE stares at him for a long time, then simply turns about and leaves in disgust)

ROBINSON: (after him) Yes, mate, me. George Augustus Robinson. Antidestinarian! Foul godless Reformation voice!
    (then to audience, indicating DOVE)
That's what you get. Stop for a brief human pause on the historical path, and they think they can take liberties. One moment in time... one... a certain day, a couple of blacks do in some white nobody, and my name is hauled over hot coals. Two years in the Flinders Island hell hole and where were those hot coals then? Nowhere! If it wasn't for me, they wouldn't even be alive to be standing trial today. And more especially with that hanging horror up on that bench with his buck teeth. I mean he's more than likely to rope me in too! Hey, hey, look, Judge, you take that Truganinni. Do you see the effort put in just with her alone? My advice... word to the wise... keep her out of your private chambers. Trouble with a capital T.

      (turns outright to confront mirror on wall)
You be the judge.
      (seems to listen to it)
And I most definitely concur.

      (He straightens his clothes, cocks his hat with a defiant flurry, then leaves the room... getting entangled again, of course, in the curtain divide.)

      <u>*Blackout.*</u>*)*

Part 3: King Billy's Bones

Hobart, 1869, during the funeral of William Lanne, or King Billy, reputed to be (certainly at the time) the last full-blooded male Tasmanian Aboriginal.

'William Lanne (King Billy), the last Tasmanian male, died in 1869 at the age of 34. She (Truganinni) thought of the deaths at Flinders Island, the horrors of the trial and executions of Port Phillip... she thought of King Billy, with his hands and feet cut off, and the skull lying on the blood-soaked earth by the broken coffin. "Don't let them cut me up", she begged as she lay dying. "Bury me behind the mountains". She was buried at Cascades, Hobart, with great precautions against the body-snatchers. Today, her bones are strung together in the Tasmanian Museum -- no longer on public view, but in a 'coffin-like' box in the basement.'

Clive Turnbull, *The Black War*

(See earlier Author's Note to Part 1: White Exercises)

List of Characters

McKAY   'authority' on Tasmanian Aborigines
GILET   his ticket-of-leave servant
DR DINGBY   general Hobart practitioner
MILLINGTON   undertaker
MOLLY   barmaid
COLVIN   whaling boat captain
TIMMS   whaling boat captain
ATWELL   colonial Under-Secretary
TRUGANINNI

Scene 1

(The drawing room of ALEXANDER McKAY, gentleman of Hobart, member of the Royal Society, authority on the Tasmanian Aborigines.

The room reflects McKay's secured position in his society. The furniture has been pushed back against the walls to make space for a table that stands in the centre of the room. On the table, and the floor underneath it, are white lilies and carnations.

McKay is finishing arranging the furniture. GILET, his servant, enters)

GILET: Dr Robert Dingby has arrived, sir.

McKAY: Send him in, send him in.
   (GILET goes to leave)
And if any other guests arrive, let them find their own way in, Gilet. Today we won't stand on formalities.
   (pause)
And don't refuse entrance to anyone. Understand?

(GILET affirms, waits, McKAY reflects)

McKAY: When the coffin comes, lend a hand, will you? And tell them to be careful. For once in his life, even though it's too late.

GILET: Shall I leave the door open then, sir?

McKAY: Best to. None may come, but then the whole town might turn out.

GILET: Front or back?

McKAY: (sharply) I said we'd stand on no ceremony.

GILET: Yes sir.

McKAY: You've seen to it that the invitation has got about?

GILET: Everybody should know about it by now, sir.

McKAY: Good, good. Send in Dr Dingby.

(Exit GILET; after a time DINGBY enters)

DINGBY: (reflecting good friends) Dr Robert Dingby, slowed by Fate, passed by time, extinguished member of the Royal College of Surgeons, London -- and I think I still remember where that is -- colonial surgeon and turned out very well because of it, has come to present his present state. How are you, my dear boy?

McKAY: Come in, Robert.

DINGBY: Bring the room to me, Alexander. You're obviously taking it somewhere.
  (noticing and touching the flowers)
With your scientific mind, what sort of insects do you expect to catch with these?

McKAY: (not wanting to be frivolous) I asked you here with good reason.

DINGBY: Ah, it's my serious friend. Alexander McKay, you were never so bluff. Nor so decorous. It must be something serious.

McKAY: Serious, interesting. Some might laugh -- certainly not many are going to lament.

DINGBY: Interesting, serious, in a fete-like arrangement. The Governor's coming, is that it?

McKAY: Damn his eyes, man. If he cared, this wouldn't be necessary.

DINGBY: No? Then it's certainly not laughable. His neglect of state is only humorous when he attends to it. What then? A theatrical performance in John Citizen's parlour?
  (pause)

Ah, I see I'm being over-flippant.

McKAY: King Billy has died.

(DINGBY glances away)

McKAY: You hear? King Billy died last night.

DINGBY: (more soberly) Last night, I know.

McKAY: The last one gone.

DINGBY: The last male surely, Alexander, but let's not forget our Queen Truganinni, though she might be of less academic interest, I'll warrant. She still warrants the mention, though, don't you think?

McKAY: He was to have been buried early this morning, but I had it postponed. Do you know why?

DINGBY: (theatrical again) Why? Alexander McKay, the best living authority on the intellectual endowments and the martial character of the now almost extinct Tasmanian Aboriginals. By right of word and interest, you have the authority. Why not you, after all? Though I'll ask. Why?

McKAY: To my knowledge, nobody knew he died last night. Nobody would have even been at his burial. No hats taken off, no standing still. King Billy, the last male gone, put away at nine and nobody the wiser. A few minutes past nine, then an end to the story?
    (pause)
We shouldn't get off so lightly. I had his burial postponed. I'm taking it on myself. Guests are coming; I've ordered my front door left open.

DINGBY: To all and their sundries?

McKAY: One burial. One decent, endorsed burial, Robert. Don't you think the race deserves that?

DINGBY: Of course. A minor request, the least, etcetera. Full rites to the ground, a spear, a waddy, union jacks, the unfurling of prayer; at last you'll see people bowing their heads over one of them. A Tasmanoid mourned. You've been trying for years.
(pause, then slyly)
But peace in the ground? That too?

McKAY: (quickly positive) Peace in the soil that we took them from.

DINGBY: But drop the last male in and just let him lay there? Don't you know how valuable the skeleton of that man is?

McKAY: (looking) Be serious, Robert.

DINGBY: I am; you've seen me so before. What is a burial when Science and Anatomy are concerned? No, I'm serious in this case. Should we dig in what shouldn't historically ever be dug in?

(McKAY is dismissive)

DINGBY: Look, a letter came to me a few months ago. It was from the Royal College, still crumbling around it's edges and I speak not of the letter's paper. I know that. But they asked of the possibility of procuring the bones of the last Tasmanian male. They want it for dangling in some corner to delight their old fools over vintage port back in London. That's all. But they want it, nonetheless.

McKAY: One decent burial, that's what he'll get.

DINGBY: No, no, you're forgetting real Science! It never even let the Industrial Revolution rest in its grave. You don't think it'll let Billy do so? Alexander?
(meaningfully)
You ask your own Royal Society.

McKAY: If they've been waiting for his death like a pack of jackals, I'll resign.

DINGBY: The Royal Society's been digging up old bones and new for years, dear boy.

McKAY: He'll have a burial, a reception of the minimum of respect! And he'll have it this afternoon.

DINGBY: And you are going to give it to him. Well, who else?, as I've said.
(losing interest)
Why did you invite me especially?

McKAY: I don't know. To help. To help me.
(looks into the flowers, then, needing assistance...)
For years now people have come to me. 'Let's talk about the Tasmanoid', they say, 'What do you know?' A night's sky is black. Some people are. I am not. That's all I've been able to say.
(then)
Yet I've dared to clear my throat and try.

DINGBY: You are the authority, Alex old son. It's that curious fame given by the Curious.

McKAY: Fame? Attachment, rather. A vulture at the end of a hardening artery. I just thought I might need a comment on this afternoon... somebody to assess it, to say how it goes off. I thought you might be interested.

DINGBY: In anatomy, Alexander. Not in absolution of consciences.

McKAY: In humanity, damn it!

DINGBY: (doing so) Well, I'll arrange the flowers. The tip, the do. I was a choir boy once. You and me together. Don't you remember?

McKAY: (morbidly) Other things have been once.

DINGBY: Alexander, dear boy, why do you tie yourself up over them so much? From the outside, it's so... impotent. I mean, why

don't you just do as most would in your position? Love the idea of them if you can't warm the flesh. After all, let's not get sordid. The world needs thinkers. I mean, where would I be without thinkers? Some of my patients I loathe the sight of. Yet I still tickle them.
 (pause)
Even now you look disgusted with yourself. Did you kill him? Did you, in your secret way, aim silver at his heart?
 (gets no answer, holds up a flower)
Why not red? More dramatic.

 (Re-enter GILET)

GILET: It's arrived, sir.

McKAY: (relieved) Is Millington there?

GILET: He brought it with him.

DINGBY: The head tucked under his arm. That's our caretaker.

McKAY: Help him bring it in, Gilet. And go carefully. It will have enough rough treatment before today is over.

 (GILET nods, goes out. McKAY and the doctor wait expectantly.

 GILET and MILLINGTON, both struggling, come in with the coffin)

MILLINGTON: (conversation for the sake of it) He's all ready as you asked, Mr McKay. He's heavy though, heavy. A strapping lad, he was. Had to use all my strength on his biceps, ha ha.

McKAY: Put him on the table there.

DINGBY: (inappropriate and knowing it) A pyre fit for a king. I'll set a match to this table leg. Alexander, you'll have your final ritual. Wilting, curing, smoked and all.

McKAY: (for himself) He'll rest in my house for a while.

DINGBY: Now you're altogether too intense, Alex. You'll have all the ladies of Hobart following you with their tongues out. Our own pale and fiendishly attractive Alexander-Hamlet mooching along the scent trail of a ghost. A thimbleful of gin, spoonfuls of Madeira and all those chasing ladies will be thinking that Alexander McKay is fading on a pine-away. All that mothering instinct; they won't be able to resist you! And all the rest of us feeling so unmercifully human by comparison.

McKAY: (strained) Robert, you are my friend.

DINGBY: Professed and admitted.

McKAY: Will you be quiet, or will I throw you out?

(DINGBY shrugs, then turns away. GILET edges off)

MILLINGTON: (evasively) I did as much as possible, sir.

McKAY: (reacting to the hint) What's wrong?

MILLINGTON: ...Nothing, Mr McKay sir.
  (then quickly)
Nothing, like. The parlour has been busy this morning. Like a weight on my mind. You understand. People die, sir.

McKAY: (quickly bitter) Yes, yes. People die. We stretch out in the final measure. The fattest, the tallest, the heaviest, and so to the shrivel. People die, well said.

DINGBY: (amused, back in game) Don't be too hard on him, Alexander. To our esteemed undertaker, it's merely guild-like observance. Isn't it somewhat similar with our own guilds as well?

McKAY: As well as what? When you go will one human direction become extinct as well? And me who's done all the talking, and Millington here who's done all the laying-out, and Gilet who's done all the running after, will some unique human pathway dry up when we go? What's taken off the sum of things when we gasp our last?

MILLINGTON: (in ignorance) Somebody has to do the arranging, sir.

McKAY: (turning on him) Today, Millington, today, between the tiresome passings that cluttered up your parlour, there has been a death that will be thought on over. And on the imagining of the scene in this room, some man some time will lay down a farthing. A farthing for its worth... next to nothing, okay. But it's still a worth, Millington. And whoever he is, he will think on past us, past the geometry of this room, past that box and he will come to a halt when he comes to the fate of a poor black man who died and cluttered up your parlour for a time there. Yes, people die, Millington, and God bless the light!

(He strides from the room)

MILLINGTON: I say something wrong, Doctor? People do die.

DINGBY: (facetiously) They do indeed, Millington. And you were quite right in saying so, my good man. The world needs thinkers, though I've just said so. Take this room, this coffin. Take the flowers, or me. Take yourself, for instance...

MILLINGTON: What have I done, sir?

DINGBY: A blush in time, all, but we have to stand firm, being victims ourselves.

MILLINGTON: (confused) Pardon?

DINGBY: (leaving) Wait here, Millington. The guests will be along in a moment. I, with God's grace and the twinkle in His eye, will to Mr McKay with verbal balm.

(DINGBY leaves.

Alone, MILLINGTON furtively goes over to ensure that the lid of the coffin is securely screwed down. While he is doing so, enter MOLLY)

MILLINGTON: (mumbling) Sometimes I wish I had some competition. I hate political copses.

MOLLY: (right behind him) What did you say?

MILLINGTON: (startled) Who are you?

MOLLY: Molly, dearie, Molly. If you don't know me, you don't listen in the nice'n'naughty places, Gawd luvya. I know who you are. Carrying on with dead bodies like you do. Shame.

MILLINGTON: (scandalized) I beg yours?

MOLLY: I haven't got one. The day's all blue outside. I got talking with a spotted dog. Old Billy would have loved today. A good day to get buried in, if you're not out working. Molly of the Dog and Partridge; you must have heard of me. I mend sailors' legs by taking out the cork.
    (winks)
I can fix them up too, given half the chance.
    (She goes over to the coffin)
Is this Billy here?
    (knocking on the top)
Is this you, Billy?
    (theatrical wait)
It's you all right. No good denying it, eh?
    (remembering something)
Wait. Wait.

(She searches in her purse, pulls out a shilling, and ceremoniously places it on top of the coffin)

MILLINGTON: What a filthy habit.'

MOLLY: Oh, I don't know about that, cock. I owe it to him in a sort of way. What I mean is, he didn't prove up to it, but he was

brave, my Billy was. He'd have a go and pay his way. Last weekend, he paid up front, like.
    (can't suppress giggle)
It must have cursed his luck. If you get over-generous, something's sure to happen. I know, I know. I'm Molly, Dog and Partridge.

MILLINGTON: (formally) How do you do?

MOLLY: Passably, they say.
    (then looking)
You must be the dirty old man who put him there.

MILLINGTON: I have only business relations with my client.

MOLLY: He was new to it, like most things, Billy was. Spotting whales. But he never got sea-sick, not Billy. I used to sing him shanties, so I ought to know. Though he was black, he was a bit of an abo. I know the type, poor lovie. You can tell by their eyes they can't leave it alone. He'd get paid, off he'd come, we'd have him at the Dog and Partridge till... till... you know what?... till some dirty dog laughed at him. And then he'd go; up and go.
    (pause)
I never come at that. The brats on the streets were the worst. They' throw rocks. I didn't come at that, neither.
    (pause)
He was not bad, Billy wasn't. He was handsome and good. Honest with money, he was. You could tell he wasn't used to it. And famous as well. Lots of things... He met Prince Alfred, f'instance. Tea and cakes and doilies to match. Billy said it was the first deck he hadn't had to scrub while he was down there on his knees. It was aboard the Royal yacht, see. It's a shame he's here.
    (She dabs her eyes)
That's why I'm here. That's his shilling, all said n' done.

MILLINGTON: I didn't mean to be inquisitive, miss. Doesn't pay in my profession.

MOLLY: You're a queer one, you are.

(pointing at the coffin)
Who's going to do you like that when the time comes?

MILLINGTON: (eagerly) Oh, I know it all off by heart!

(Then realizes, when she laughs, he's said something foolish. He turns away and sulks. MOLLY walks around the coffin, as though there might be a peek-hole in it.

Re-enter DINGBY, effects 'love at first sight')

DINGBY: An apparition. A vision. Venus unthroned. Stop exactly where you are.

MOLLY: Oh, it's you.

DINGBY: Me, my chick-a-dee.

MOLLY: (petulantly) Hoi, I've come to be solemn. My friend is in here.

DINGBY: Millington?

MOLLY: No, just resting.

(and laughs raucously)

DINGBY: ('rising' to her) What a coincidence! Millington, my dear chap, truth and lies here do dovetail and pattern. This sweet, once dear and still costly creature is here because of Billy's mind. I am here for his body. You are here for what you can get out of laying both to rest. What a travelling troupe we three would make! And he, how our King Billy has danced to our tune!
  (to MOLLY)
Ah, angel, the thoughts you inspire.

MOLLY: (sulkily) I've come to be respectable, not talk to gentlemen.

MILLINGTON: Dr Dingby. Miss. Please. Decorum.

DINGBY: Millington is right. Undertakers invariably are in the end.

(Pause)

MOLLY: Come and have a look.
(to MILLINGTON)
You too. come on. For him, just a peep. Come on, old Bill won't bite.

(The three gather to look for a solemn moment over the coffin)

DINGBY: Far away. A memory already.

MOLLY: (softly) Kids would throw stones at him.

DINGBY: (but with wider meaning) Foreshadowing the surgeon's cold mind?

MOLLY: All kids are like that, little buggers.

DINGBY: And men with scalpels.

MOLLY: (looking at him sharply) What d'you mean?

DINGBY: (too innocently) Why, the word, that's all, my chuck. 'Scalpels'. Have you ever rolled it around your tongue and noticed the way it rattles... oh, yes, rather, rattles... about one's head? Scalpels is an incisive word, scalpels is. It comes from the word scalp, I imagine and appropriately.

(The others don't even pretend to know what he is talking about, even more so that he has become quite serious.

DINGBY shrugs, tries to laugh his way out of it)

DINGBY: Well, what's deemed fashionable must be done or by God the board of governors of the old Society will burp his annoyance very rudely and loudly across the whole of London. Wouldn't want our Billy to cause a gush like that.

(Enter the two whaling boat captains COLVIN and TIMMS.

DINGBY welcomes them, almost rudely)

DINGBY: Why, gentlemen, whoever or whatever you are, you're the perfect guests. Come in, come in. Seat yourselves for the showing. If you're good at arranging flowers, you might make yourselves useful in the meantime.

COLVIN: (gruffly) We heard of the invitation.

DINGBY: To be sure.

TIMMS: Is that Billy?

DINGBY: He's the only guest that has not said so.

(COLVIN and TIMMS don't take kindly to his supercilious attitude. They go over to the coffin. They openly inspect it before:)

COLVIN: (suspiciously) Where is McKay?

DINGBY: The deceased was one of your crew, I gather?

MILLINGTON: (disapprovingly) He was. They engage half-castes as well.

DINGBY: And still bring in whales? That harpoon's extremely well...
    (for phonetic)
 ...cast.

COLVIN: (brushing that aside) Where is Mr McKay in all this?

DINGBY: The invitation was only for poor Billy. Mr McKay is very much alive. When his day comes you'll hear in good time; I shouldn't worry.

MOLLY: (playfully) I'll be here too if he gives me fair warning.

DINGBY: Alexander McKay won't die without completing arrangements, sweet girl. Invitations will go out, signed by his own hand. Just listen for the bells, and RSVP. as soon as you can.

MOLLY: You are a fool.

DINGBY: A doctor second. In order of merit.

COLVIN: (scornfully) Is this a funeral?

DINGBY: (amused) Not due to begin for another few seconds. I believe the guest of honour is here, but not the toaster. Until he charges us to fill our glasses, I hope you'll forgive a man for working up a little tickle of a thirst.

COLVIN: (booming) I said where's McKay?

McKAY: Here.

(They turn. McKAY, with GILET, has entered the room.

He shakes the Captains' hands, which they give grudgingly)

McKAY: You must be Colvin and Timms. I hear you treated Billy kindly, so thank you for that.
    (to GILET)
Do we expect any more to arrive?
    (GILET shakes his head)
Right, we'll begin then. Who's to carry with me?

COLVIN: (cutting him short) Wait a minute, McKay.

TIMMS: It's a decent thing you're doing for Billy, but there's just one thing we'd like to know...

COLVIN: ... why are you doing this?

TIMMS: Aye, we'll have an answer before you go on.

McKAY: Who else, if not me? Some government clerk?

COLVIN: Us! We'll break our backs carrying the lad alone, if need be. We'll hear the truth and either leave or join you.

McKAY: (impatiently) You may leave or join us, as you wish. That coffin is mine.

COLVIN: (really aggressive) But not what's in it, McKay.

McKAY: Come or go, either way.

TIMMS: We'll stay only if it's not a vain show, McKay.

McKAY: Good. We're going to need all the hands we can get.

COLVIN: Then open that box. We'll have a look inside.

McKAY: (arrested) What? What did you say?

TIMMS: We're sea captains. McKay. Before we join a ship, we'll look inside her.

McKAY: Have you gone quite mad?

COLVIN: (booming) Will you open that box, or will I tear it apart?

McKAY: No! I'll leave that to God. Now get out of my house!

(TIMMS sees MILLINGTON trying to edge off. He catches the undertaker, and twists his ear)

TIMMS: Your rats are deserting McKay.

MILLINGTON: (squirming) Why me?

TIMMS: Tell us, what have you and your friends done with our boy in there. We'll hear it out of your own mouth, then we'll leave you all alone. To talk and be damned.

McKAY: You're speaking nonsense!

MILLINGTON: (hysterically) I do what I'm told to!

TIMMS: (twisting harder) More!

MILLINGTON: Lamp and shades'. Mr McKay...!

(Enter ATWELL, the Colonial Under-Secretary)

ATWELL: (impeccably) Now, now, Captain Timms, release that creature. You will have to be in his hands too one day.

McKAY: Atwell.

ATWELL: I see I've come at just the right time, Alexander.

DINGBY: (oddly bitter) Ah, the government imprint has arrived. See the tortoise behind its shell. Slow moving but well cased in.

ATWELL: Ever observant, Doctor Dingby.

DINGBY: But, my dear Atwell, you are dressed for important work. The tie, the suit, the brolly, the felt hat; it's all so meaningfully drab.

ATWELL: It's not my best finery, I grant you.

TIMMS: Official or not, Mr Atwell?

ATWELL: Alas, Captain, with service for the public, one is never off duty. I'm always glad to be amongst friends, though. And on rare occasions that gives me the chance to indulge my natural curiosity.
    (meaningfully to DINGBY)
Doctor, you should know.

DINGBY: (strangely uncomfortable) There is a ring of novelty in this situation, I agree.

(And turns away 'into' himself)

TIMMS: (had enough) Come on, Colvin.

McKAY: Wait!
   (turning to ATWELL)
You are here officially. That's obvious. What isn't is why?

ATWELL: The Governor's discretion and, I confess, his slight bemusement. After all, Alexander, the government was to pay for the burial, but at nine o'clock this morning. Not now and not here. You see our problem?

McKAY: The same cost to bury a pauper, nothing more.

ATWELL: But nothing less.

McKAY: A few formalities fit for a human being that's what I expect from a government that's never done anything for them before.
   (then to COLVIN and TIMMS)
You came here because of something you heard. I know nothing of this.

TIMMS: (looking) Perhaps you don't.

McKAY: What was it?

TIMMS: It's got around that Billy has been tampered with, McKay. That more than his clothes were taken off him.

(McKAY turns sharply towards ATWELL who does not commit himself. He then moves towards MILLINGTON)

McKAY: Millington?

MILLINGTON: (backing off) I only do a job, Mr McKay.' I've got no competition, see!

McKAY: Open that coffin.

(MILLINGTON looks towards ATWELL)

McKAY: OPEN THAT COFFIN!

(MILLINGTON is jolted towards the box)

MOLLY: 'Ere, is that allowed? I mean, would you like it?

DINGBY: It's a question of property, not propriety, my dear. The bird may have flown his coop or gone to seed. It's better to be sure.

MOLLY: But that's my Billy in there! That's my shilling on top. How would you like it? How would you like to be caught in a position like that?

McKAY: (to MILLINGTON) Get a move on.

(Finally, MILLINGTON gets the coffin lid loosened.)

McKAY moves forward as do the others. He opens the coffin.

A general recoil. MOLLY turns away, gulps back nausea)

McKAY: (stunned, staring) My God, my God.

COLVIN: (to ATWELL) I should tear your bloody heart out for this.

McKAY: You're in on this, Atwell?

ATWELL: Officially, that's all. I was sent here to prevent just this sort of thing, Alexander. Please calm down, all of you.

(His normally overbearing manner is just right for this occasion. They all stop to gather themselves)

TIMMS: (quietly) He was a fine young man with arms as strong as any's. He would have bred had girls survived for him. I had a photograph taken of him last year. It was 'too' black for him, he said. Too black' for him. We had him thinking that way. That was a crime.

McKAY: (almost deadpan at ATWELL) You've stumped his legs and cut off his hands. Why not his heart? Why not his... personals? And why his skull as well, when so warm, Atwell, when it must have still been warm? Answer me that, Atwell. Why butcher him? You're not going to answer?

ATWELL: (finally) The Governor is sorry for what has been necessary. Let me explain...

DINGBY: (genuinely, to McKAY) No, don't turn away, Alexander. Atwell is right. We run and walk in this world, but one or two of us do so watched. King Billy was one. King Billy and his life; it's been ours right from the start. Think on it. He himself knew he was a public performance.

ATWELL: Millington, go and get a seal. No one else must open this coffin again.
  (MILLINGTON leaves gladly. To McKAY)
Your own Royal Society thought our museum should have Billy's bones. They petitioned the Governor demanding the right of the skeleton. He agreed in principle over other institutions that made applications but not in fact. In other words, your colleagues...

McKAY: No longer my colleagues.

ATWELL: ... your Royal Society colleagues were told that if any one group should have the bones it should be them, yes... but since no one group could, their claim was denied.

McKAY: What about me?

ATWELL: The Governor would bank on Billy being safe in your hands, Alexander.
  (then looking meaningfully at DINGBY)
It seems that our other scientific institutions were after the corpse as well. Is that not so, Dr Dingby?

DINGBY: (not now taken aback) Mr Atwell, sir, you're a crafty rascal. I had to make enquiries for my College of Surgeons, yes. Wonderful great bellies, the bunch of them. An oath of allegiance stretches out into the colony's way, sir. Which shows it up for its own stupidity, I agree.

ATWELL: Well put.

DINGBY: Not well put enough to secure Billy boy.

ATWELL: That is right, too.
    (turns back to McKAY)
Alexander, last night while the body lay in hospital, its head was skinned and the skull removed. We don't know who by but
    (pointing to the coffin)
that one you see in there, ill fitting, was from a dead white man who had his skull similarly removed. You perhaps will grant the Governor had to act quickly. It was obvious that somebody wanted the skull to blackmail us for the rest of the skeleton. Crude but effective. After all, what good is a skeleton without its head? As worthless as one without hands or feet. As your Royal Society friends were quick to point out. They feared body-snatching for the rest of the body in the grave tonight. So they re-petitioned the Governor and reminded him of his decree. Under sanction, therefore, they were allowed to remove what they called 'the extremities'. Hands and feet to us. They've been stored in a safe place, the Governor is told.
    (pause)
It is now hoped that whoever took the skull will realize it to be as worthless as a part of a body sans 'extremities', and hence return it.

McKAY: You people, you want to carve up everything we kill?

ATWELL: (kindly) Not that.

McKAY: (to DINGBY) What did you know of this?

DINGBY: Only what was pre-ordained, Alexander.

McKAY: (nodding, quietening) You warned me.

DINGBY: I did, my friend.

(GILET comes into the room)

GILET: There's one more outside, sir. Shall I let her in.

McKAY: More's the point: will they let us out?
(then)
No, Gilet, nobody else.

GILET: (intimately) She's the one you wanted me to keep a lookout for, sir.

McKAY: (reacting) Truganinni! Bring her in! Close that coffin, quickly!

DINGBY: Why, haven't they met?

McKAY: Fool! Fool!

ATWELL: Do it, Gilet.

(GILET hurries to attend to the coffin, but is fumbling. He stops inexplicably when TRUGANINNI enters.

She is now nearing seventy years old... an old lady. She shuffles over to the coffin, looks down at it, then backs away to a chair. She does not speak, and sits, staring ahead with little involvement.

The others watch, then seem to forget about her.

COLVIN brings their attentions back to the coffin.)

COLVIN: He was our boy, the top-of-the-mast man. They don't come often, not as good as that. Something about being black; he could see a whale when it wasn't there for us. One of the best.

MOLLY: He always paid, if not beforehand.

TIMMS: (at her) Aye. He knew you, too. You're from the Dog and Partridge. He was a bit of a young stallion. He would've known you.

MOLLY: He'd try, try. I'll grant you that.

COLVIN: Though a black first, he was a sailor first, mark.

TIMMS: No, man... I reckoned a black first, a sailor after. Strange that, strange.

COLVIN: It didn't worry me. Nor him. Nor none, well enough. When they got t'know him.

TIMMS: You'd see his old crony women ...
    (indicating TRUGANINNI)
like her, poking and scratching, laughing at him. Him asking could any of them have kids because he's just found out he's the only man left.

(pause)

Further back too. He'd tell us things. A boy, taking his first steps, his mother laying a lizard across the palm of his hand, and humming to him:
Be good
Be kind
Do not touch things that belong to others.
Do not touch any such thing.
Be good.
Be kind.

COLVIN: Aye, there were the songs, one or two. To warm the night. He was scared of the sea. But his eyesight was good, and so were his songs.

McKAY: (painfully) We won't wait any longer.

(Re-enter MILLINGTON with wax and an old brass stamp)

MILLINGTON: I couldn't find a seal, sir.

ATWELL: Then what is that?

MILLINGTON: A brass stamp from out of our dispensary.

(looking at it oddly)
I think.

ATWELL: (impatiently) Has it got a pattern?

MILLINGTON: (nodding) I can't make out what it is.

ATWELL: It will do. Just get on.

(MILLINGTON applies the wax in several places. He presses on the stamp, looks, and takes an involuntary step backwards. Laughs weakly)

ATWELL: What is it now, man?

MILLINGTON: (apologetically) It was all I could find, Mr Atwell.

(DINGBY pushes the undertaker to one side, and looks at the seal)

DINGBY: (with hard humour) Alexander, this is for your sense of the dramatic. Look, man. The carcass is finally branded by the sole claimant owner...

(McKAY looks)

McKAY: (incredulous) 'World'...?

DINGBY: Fire on fire, dear boy. There it is. 'World'. You have your answer. Much more than Atwell could possibly say.

TIMMS: Move him, McKay! Here's my shoulder!

COLVIN: And mine for pity, man!

McKAY: Take him, take him away.

(COLVIN, TIMMS, GILET and MILLINGTON hoist up the box. They leave. The others follow one by one.

TRUGANINNI gets up lifelessly. As she walks past McKAY, he stops her)

ROBINSON: Truganinni, will you stay here with me? A guest in my house, Truganinni. You can rest here as long as you like.

(After a time, TRUGANINNI looks up, nods casually, then shuffles out after the others.

McKAY follows)

Scene 2

(Next day. The furniture returned to its usual place.

McKAY is sitting looking at the table.

Enter ATWELL)

McKAY: (rising) Mr Under-Secretary ... you've caught me unprepared. Where is Gilet?

ATWELL: I brought something of yours with me. He's helping with it. A good man, that Gilet. Have you thought of his parole?

McKAY: He's safe enough here. A servant of the state, but he's better as a friend of mine.

ATWELL: Yes, of course.
   (pause)
You're looking tired, Alexander.

McKAY: I tried to do something yesterday. A quip, a gesture; more than I should, I suppose. Today, I have a strong sense of failure.

ATWELL: Other people have never had your interest in the race, that's all. To them, the Tasmanian was an oddity -- King Billy, therefore, a show piece.

McKAY: (bitterness rising again) As vague as that? You know better.

ATWELL: Perhaps.

McKAY: Objects of lust, savages to hate or fear, then scavengers of contempt. In that order, the history of the Tasmanians. And now they are gone, objects of derision. Not even allowed to go to their Maker whole. A few dangling loose ends. About seventy-five years, that's all they could stand us. They simply laid down to die, Atwell, and I fancy that's an adequate commentary on us when all's said and done.

ATWELL: You're a funny man, Alexander. Still, your efforts do not go unnoticed. You're a humanitarian, and people are looking to you for that. As an official, I can say it with knowledge. By the way, you have Truganinni staying here with you?

McKAY: I am harbouring her, yes.

ATWELL: Watch over her closely. Mobs would claw past you just to see her now. Being the last, she's doubly unique. That makes people doubly insistent.

McKAY: I'll watch over her.

ATWELL: As we all know you will.
    (indicating intention of leaving)
Well ...

McKAY: What did you say you had for me?

ATWELL: I'll see to it on my way out. It was nothing important.

McKAY: (knowingly) If you have the coffin outside, let them bring it in.

ATWELL: (shrewdly) You've heard?

McKAY: Nothing. You've changed your manner. That could only mean one thing. Yesterday, I actually thought I could give him peace in the ground.

ATWELL: After yesterday ... I don't think I can bring myself to tell you.

McKAY: I am no dried-boned optimist. They can bring it in.

(ATWELL leaves the room, calls, then re-enters.

Enter GILET and another man carrying an empty coffin. They set it down, then leave quickly.

McKAY goes over to look at it)

McKAY: Quite, quite empty. Did he ever exist? King Billy, the last hope, vanished.
 (fiercely)
I felt so sure I could prevent this. I felt I could ...
 (stops)
I can't even remember what I felt I could do. Maybe shame them.

ATWELL: The grave was found disturbed this morning. I was called. The earth had been removed and the coffin partly hoisted up. On the ground nearby, that skull, the substituted one. Everything around was saturated with blood. The constable swore he was asleep and heard nothing. I could have him broken, but what's the use?

McKAY: Where ...?

ATWELL: Where is the body? It may not even be in fat form by now. A trail of blood ran from the grave to one of the gates. But, for all purposes, King Billy has been snatched -- minus his hands, his feet, his skull, minus his dignity. What else ...

TRUGANINNI: AIEE!

(She stumbles into the room. For a moment she rocks, hugging herself, in a kneeling position, then fully collapses in a faint)

McKAY: My God, she heard you!

(They go over and try to pick her up.

Blackout)

Scene 3

(The living room. A week later. McKAY and DINGBY)

McKAY: How serious is it?

DINGBY: My dear friend, I'm only a doctor, and a pretty crude one at that. I've helped to fashion the times but not once have I healed it. That's Robert Dingby.

McKAY: There must be something wrong with her, man.

DINGBY: (shrugging) The Tasmanoid has been going off like this for seventy-five years and we still don't know why.

McKAY: With Billy, it was diarrhea.

DINGBY: Choleraic diarrhea. With the others, mainly consumption. But these are only symptoms. It's the way the symptoms materialize and refuse to respond.

McKAY: She refuses food.

DINGBY: She's dying, Alexander.

McKAY: (stopping) Is that what you honestly think?

DINGBY: She's dying, I know.

McKAY: But what of, man, what of?

(no reply)

I had to pick her up of this very floor that day. Atwell came to her feet. Bloody fool that I was. I tried to lift her from under the armpits. The only thing that gave was her dress. She looked like she was staring up at me, unblinking, spittle running from her mouth. She kept frothing and when she awoke, kept wringing her hands.

(pause)

An hour later, probably more, she finally stopped. The other day, she went to go out into the street. There was that crowd still outside, waiting for her. When I heard the screams she made, Gilet had to haul her back. But that's not even over. That lack of movement in her legs.

DINGBY: Anything particular she talks about?

McKAY: (with shame) I can't seem to go in to see her.

DINGBY: You're doing enough, Alexander. Don't worry.

McKAY: Are you absolutely positive you can't help her?

DINGBY: Me? I'm one of those who has already done his worst.

McKAY: (suddenly fierce) Have you ever thought what it must be like to be a biological freak? A joke of Nature?

DINGBY: She is dying. The answer is there. Why should she act the tragedienne?

McKAY: You think that's what she's thinking?

DINGBY: What else?

McKAY: It's not necessary. Not here. Not in my house, Robert.

(Pause)

DINGBY: I can't give you that guarantee, Alexander.

McKAY: I only wanted it confirmed.

DINGBY: It'll be as long as she sees fit.

McKAY: (suddenly) I want her story!
(pause)
I want her story, Robert.

DINGBY: You think she will give it to you?

(McKAY shrugs)

DINGBY: If she would tell it, I suppose it Could do you both good. I knew a minstrel once. He was always after stories. He'd sing them once and then never use them again. Sucked the goodness out of them, he said.

McKAY: (quiet determination) She must give it to me.

DINGBY: Bring her in here. It's bright enough and cool. And central; it'll be a part payment in return for you. Well, I'm off, dear boy. I've got an appointment with a certain Molly, currently of the Dog and Partridge. She uses better medicine than I could prescribe myself, and I really do need the cheering. You and your damn over-compassion, parches the throat. I think you're after a hounding for us all.

McKAY: (caustically) Before you go, how is your College of Surgeons going to feel about this?

DINGBY: I tell you frankly, there'll be some interest as before. Star attractions only last until the next one comes along. Back in London town, I can see the advertisements already starting to be put up. I'd rather be here. At least there's lamentation here.

McKAY: Yes, I am lamenting. I feel it's all my fault.

DINGBY: No, stop that.

(He turns to leave, stops)

DINGBY: She's got the death-wish, Alexander. With that story, don't wait too long.

(He leaves, McKAY sits silently for a while, then:)

McKAY: (calling) Gilet?

(GILET enters)

McKAY: Ask Truganinni to come in here. No, tell her and move her things in here.

(Blackout)

Scene 4

(TRUGANINNI sits half-propped on a sofa. She is staring at the wall. Some untouched food is on the tray beside her.

Note: The shadow play of a large crowd outside can be seen through the window. Throughout this scene, the shadows get larger; they spread more and more across the floor towards her.

Enter McKAY. He does so tentatively. Though she hears him, she doesn't look around)

McKAY: There's food beside you, Truganinni.
   (no reaction)
There are some questions about food, but not about what it's for. How are you feeling?
   (offering hand)
Would you like to try and walk today? Try. You don't you're your legs going, you know that.
   (a dismissive pause)
I said, would you like to try and walk, Truganinni?

TRUGANINNI: (into air, almost lullaby) A ridge of sand and animal droppings. If it was only me, I would be glad. If it was only me, I would dance on an empty belly. I would dance for my father.

McKAY: Try to walk. Outside, even when it's raining, people stand waiting for you. They'll give you cheer.

TRUGANINNI: (rocking) Oi... oi...

McKAY: What's the matter? They know you're in my house, so why don't you look out?
   (pause)
You're safe here. I'm here. Don't you know, want to know, me?

TRUGANINNI: (into air) At night, my father would light his fire at a place apart. My mother comes singing to him. I hear her scream, and deep by my stick I finger the yams...

McKAY: Here, your red handkerchief. You wear it when you're out walking in town. Remember.
   (then directive)
Just make yourself remember.

TRUGANINNI: If I was alone, I would dance empty-bellied. Hands on my belly.

McKAY: Truganinni!

TRUGANINNI: (languid) What do you want with me?

McKAY: You are a guest in my house.

TRUGANINNI: I know.

McKAY: Just try to get better.

   (TRUGANINNI begins to hum)

McKAY: You needn't keep yourself sick. What's the point? Not... here. Why here?
   (she hums over him)
On your life, are any of us here running you down now?

(she stops humming, thinks on that)
Am I running you down now? Is anyone here?

TRUGANINNI: (flinging question back) Why are you running us down? Why are you running us down, white man?
(just as suddenly returns to crooning)
A ridge of sand and animal droppings.

McKAY: Eat some food. Sleep, sleep.
(gets annoyed at continuing no reaction)
Will-you-take-some- food?

(He is about to give up, when:)

TRUGANINNI: (laconic) You have gone to trouble.

McKAY: No.

TRUGANINNI: The killing is finished with. You will tell me that.

McKAY: A few mouthfuls, and you'll be back to your old self. A little pot of ale, hmm?

(TRUGANINNI turns her eyes to the wall)

TRUGANINNI: The fire would be lit; though in the air would be... whisperings sss sss.

(The shadows of the crowd outside swell; the people asking to see her become audible. She shudders.)

TRUGANINNI: Don't let them in until I am far away.

McKAY: Don't stay sick or I must, Truganinni.

TRUGANINNI: Oi, they will come...

(Noise of crowd fades a little. In the lull...)

McKAY: They wait outside all our doors. Eventually. One door to one man. There shouldn't be more, Truganinni. My own will come soon enough. Walk out from here. Don't let there be so many outside my door.

(*But she remains with face averted. He speaks to her of his own guilt; he wants her to understand*)

McKAY: Listen. Listen... there runs one of your women with a belly bulge in front. I'm too young to know what it is. She can't escape so she climbs a tree. I was only a lad and I shoot at her, laughing. And then the scream. When I open my eyes, a foetus drops, bounces at my feet... then her... I think it was my father's gun! *I think it was me!*

(*He stops, shocked by the confession. After the silence that follows...*)

TRUGANINNI: What do you care?

McKAY: One day, they'll be waiting outside for me. I will die with it.

TRUGANINNI: Who will care?

McKAY: Let me save you from this!'

TRUGANINNI: Will you make love to me, white man, give me presents? I am dirty down there; there has been plenty of company.

McKAY: Old woman, when your people were being shot at, I went out to try conciliation. You know that; you were with Robinson. I did my best to make it up what I did. But I swear I didn't do it just to send you all to die on that island. Nobody could say I did that.
    (pause, then)
But who would say that I didn't? Would you? Will you stand up for me and say that I didn't, Truganinni?
    (she refuses to reply)

If you won't, then nobody will. You know that. All right, old woman, I fired a bullet. But I was young. Don't you see? None of you ever said to me, all right Alexander McKay, you've made it up, go your way. *None.* Why can't you? Now. The last. Just say it. Will it kill you to say it?

(He is drowned out by the mob outside surging again. The shadows inch towards TRUGANINNI. She moans)

McKAY: (heavily accusing her) What do you want? More of my ridicule than even King Billy's funeral? Are you wishing another Billy on me, old woman?

(The crowd momentarily drowns him out. Now she is almost opening reversing things and pointing it out to him.

He has to shout to be heard now)

McKAY: You should answer me something. I'm involved, Truganinni, but don't let all the plays end with me.

TRUGANINNI: (sing-song) My legs were not strong enough to keep them away. My mother is dead when she speaks to my father. The waratah is wild and the ferns, my ferns ... oi, why should I always be afraid? It is finished ago.

McKAY: (actually getting furious) I've asked you here; you owe me something. Those people outside know you're in my house. You must walk out of here!

TRUGANINNI: (outcry) Don't let them cut me up!

(The sound of the crowd rises to crescendo)

McKAY: Give me your word you will walk out of my house

TRUGANINNI: Don't let them cut me up! Bury me behind the mountains!

McKAY: *Don't do this in my house!*

(Crowd noise and shadows cut off suddenly.

TRUGANINNI cringes into her blankets.

In the contrasting lull, McKAY waits for a reaction from her, gets none, then finally, with great heaviness, gestures disassociation)

McKAY: So. The Tasmanians die...

(He leaves her)

TRUGANINNI begins to hum softly. The crowd surges again; its shadows envelope her while she is very alone.

<u>Blackout</u>*)*

www.ingramcontent.com/pod-product-compliance
Lightning Source LLC
LaVergne TN
LVHW051655080426
835511LV00017B/2590